LOOKING REALITY IN THE EYE

Looking Reality in the Eye
MUSEUMS AND SOCIAL RESPONSIBILITY

Edited by Robert R. Janes and Gerald T. Conaty

© 2005 by Robert R. Janes and
Gerald T. Conaty

Published by the
University of Calgary Press
2500 University Drive NW
Calgary, Alberta, Canada T2N 1N4
www.uofcpress.com

No part of this publication may be reproduced, stored in a retrieval system or transmitted, in any form or by any means, without the prior written consent of the publisher or a licence from The Canadian Copyright Licensing Agency (Access Copyright). For an Access Copyright licence, visit www.accesscopyright.ca or call toll free to 1-800-893-5777.

We acknowledge the financial support of the Government of Canada through the Book Publishing Industry Development Program (BPIDP), the Alberta Foundation for the Arts and the Alberta Lottery Fund—Community Initiatives Program for our publishing activities. We acknowledge the support of the Canada Council for the Arts for our publishing program.

LIBRARY AND ARCHIVES CANADA
CATALOGUING IN PUBLICATION

Looking reality in the eye : museums and social responsibility / edited by Robert R. Janes and Gerald T. Conaty.

Co-published by: Museums Association of Saskatchewan.
Includes bibliographical references and index.
ISBN 1-55238-143-9

1. Museums—Social aspects.   I. Janes, Robert R.   II. Conaty, Gerald Thomas, 1953–   III. Museums Association of Saskatchewan.

AM7.L66 2005   069   C2005-900974-8

Cover design, Mieka West.
Internal design & typesetting, zijn digital.

This book is printed on acid-free paper. ∞

This book is dedicated to all those museum workers who are playing the edge of discontent, with the hope of transformation.

True growth is the ability of a society to transfer increasing amounts of attention and energy from the material side of life to the nonmaterial side, and thereby to advance its culture, capacity for compassion, sense of community, and strength of democracy.
— Arnold J. Toynbee, *A Study of History*

TABLE OF CONTENTS

Acknowledgments   xi

Introduction   1
Robert R. Janes and Gerald T. Conaty

History is as History Does: The Evolution of a Mission-driven Museum   19
Ruth J. Abram

Our Story in Our Words: Diversity and Equality in the Glenbow Museum   43
Gerald T. Conaty and Beth Carter

One National Museum's Work to Develop a New Model of National Service: A Work in Progress   59
Joanne DiCosimo

Engaging Young Minds and Spirits: The Glenbow Museum School   71
Michèle Gallant and Gillian Kydd

Liberty Science Center in the United States: A Mission Focused on External Relevance   85
Emlyn H. Koster and Stephen H. Baumann

Is Art Good for You?   113
Susan Pointe

Negotiating a Sustainable Path: Museums and Societal Therapy   129
Glenn C. Sutter and Douglas Worts

Out of Sight, Out of Mind: Human Remains at the Auckland Museum – Te Papa Whakahiku   153
Paul Tapsell

Telling It Like It Is: The Calgary Police Service Interpretive Centre   175
Janet Pieschel

Contributors   187

Index   191

ACKNOWLEDGMENTS

The co-editors are indebted to a number of individuals and organizations for making this book possible. Most importantly, we thank all of the authors for their contributions to this volume, especially in light of the relentless demands on their time and attention. All of them have given freely of their thoughts and experiences, and for this we are grateful.

The idea for this book emerged from a panel presentation on museums and social responsibility at the annual meeting of the Canadian Museums Association in 2002. We thank Janet Pieschel for co-organizing this panel with the senior co-editor, as well as the Canadian Museums Association for the opportunity to present this topic to our museum colleagues. Bryan H. Massam deserves special mention for his initial encouragement and support.

Walter Hildebrandt, Director of the University of Calgary Press, has been supportive of this project from the outset, and we thank him for valuing our work. John King and Windsor Viney at the University of Calgary Press were most helpful with the myriad details of manuscript preparation. We also want to thank the anonymous reviewers for their valuable insights, as well as the Glenbow Museum (Calgary, Alberta) and Parks Canada for providing essential technical support in compiling this volume in an electronic format. Joan Kanigan-Fairen and the Board of Directors of the Museums Association of Saskatchewan deserve special mention for assisting with the costs of publication.

Finally, our thanks go to our immediate families – Gwyn, Niall, Priscilla, Peter and Erica – for their unfailing encouragement and support.

Robert R. Janes
Canmore, Alberta

Gerald T. Conaty
Calgary, Alberta

February 2005

INTRODUCTION

Robert R. Janes and Gerald T. Conaty

"... for what worked yesterday becomes the gilded cage of today."
Peter Block (2002: 31)

WHAT WAS OLD IS NEW AGAIN

The idea that museums should serve a social purpose is not a new concept. Modern museology has its roots in the "cabinets of curiosities" that were developed by the gentry during the Age of Discovery (fourteenth to sixteenth centuries) and those collections that were owned by the state were often used for larger, ideological purposes.

Museums are the products of the society that supports them. Although the concept of a museum can be traced to ancient Greece, the philosophy and purpose of contemporary museums were shaped in eighteenth-century Europe. It is important to note these historical developments if we are to understand and appreciate the enduring role of museums as social institutions.

As the Age of Discovery made Europeans aware of the vastness and diversity of the world that lay beyond the continental boundaries, the explorers of these new worlds brought back samples of natural and human phenomena for those who had financed the expeditions. These collections were often housed in rooms filled with "cabinets of curiosities" where the gentry could reflect upon the strange wonders of the world.

This structure began to change near the end of the eighteenth century. With the French Revolution, collections that had belonged to the Crown, the Church, and the aristocracy became the property of the State (Grasset 1996: 190) and were put on exhibit for all the people of France. The Decree of July 27, 1793, opened the Louvre and guaranteed that the people of France would have the right of access to the collections. Later, as Napoleon I (1804–15) conquered most of Europe and North Africa, his plunder was brought back to France and housed in museums throughout the country. Collections which initially served as mementos of the past and evidence of present wealth soon became objects of study, sources of patriotism, and a medium for post-Revolutionary propaganda.

In Britain, the creation of a national collection began earlier, with the founding of the British Museum. But real democratization of museums in Britain lagged behind developments elsewhere, as conservative opinion reacted to the revolutionary attitudes of the Continent. Access to the national collection continued to be restricted to those who were acceptable (i.e., aristocratic men). However, by the 1850s a new role of civic responsibility was emerging for museums in Britain (Bennett 1996). The gentry believed that if museums were opened for public access, labourers would eschew the local tavern for a chance to ponder the art and artifacts of Western civilizations. Time spent in such contemplation was thought to lead to character reformation and a general improvement in the nature of the working class.

Museums continue to have an important social role and their underlying message has come to reflect the value of progress. Often this message is conveyed most effectively through the use of the ethnological collections, where the inevitability of progress emerges from cross-cultural comparisons.

As both Cameron (1971) and Ames (1992) observe, the creation of these public collections had a profound effect on the meaning embedded within them:

> ... the public ... came to believe that they had the right to expect that the collections would present and interpret the world in some way consistent with the values they held to be good, with the collective representations they held to be appropriate, and with the view of social reality they held to be true. (Ames 1992: 21)

Museums, thus, became temples of the dominant society (Cameron 1971: 17), reifying its principles and beliefs. They became places where the individual could compare his/her private view of reality with the view held by society in general. It is important to remember, however, that this reality had been constructed by the educated classes of society and that the perceptions of more marginal groups were mostly excluded from this reality.

PURPOSE AND SUSTAINABILITY

Just as today's societies are incredibly diverse and complex, museums are no longer the monolithic institutions of the past. Instead, many are focusing their efforts more narrowly, telling particular stories with larger meanings. Often, these stories reflect issues and people that have been marginalized by mainstream society – First Nations, immigrants, and chronic illness. This approach can also lead to an activism that embraces community issues and aspirations, in an effort to provide value and meaning.

This book is about the search for meaning among a group of museums, science centres and art galleries, at a time when many of these institutions worldwide are struggling to maintain their stability in the face of the complex challenges of the non-profit world.[1] These challenges range from declining attendance to finding the appropriate balance between public funding and earned revenues, and none of them are easily overcome. At the same time, a growing number of these museums are moving beyond the imperatives of the marketplace, with its preoccupation with money and efficiency, to embrace activities that are seemingly remote from the bottom line. Although the reasons for this are as varied as the articles in this book, there are several troublesome aspects of our contemporary world that help to make sense of this emerging search for significance in the museum world.

The contemporary search for meaning is in part a reaction to various scientific, technological and societal developments, and it is useful to consider how these facts and events have converged over time to provoke the institutional responses chronicled in this book. The story begins long ago, with one observer (McKibben 2003: 15) noting that meaning in human life has been in decline for a very long time, almost since the beginning of Western civilization. This is in contrast to our hunting and gathering ancestors whose world and its inhabitants, be they plant, animal or mineral, were saturated with meaning. Consider the Pawnee account of the Great Council of Animals, as an example (Brown 1989: 124). This Council meets in perpetual session in a cave under a round mountain, and monitors the affairs of humans wherever they may be on Earth. If a man or woman is in need or in trouble, and seeks aid with humility, the Council will choose one of its appropriate members – whether winged, four-legged, or crawling – who will then appear to the man or woman and give something of its own power, or present advice, that should thereafter guide the person's life. Human wholeness, and hence meaning, thus depend on a receptiveness to the potentialities and mysteries of the natural world. Today, Western society looks on the same landscape and deems it deaf and dumb, or else sees a treasure trove of resources and feels little or no obligation for collective responsibility. The widespread belief that nature exists to serve the interests of people has eroded much of what our species once found meaningful.

This belief in humankind's dominion over plants and animals is also the rationale for extracting wealth at the expense of the environment, yet another expression of our preoccupation with money as the measure of worth. This sentiment is now fully installed in the boardrooms of many cultural institutions, with *The Toronto Star* (Hume 2000) reporting that "the gap between the haves and the have nots of the museum world will be greater than ever." The Director of the Museum of Modern Art in New York is quoted as saying, "If you want to stay competitive in the cultural arena, you can only do it by investing large sums. That means you have to spend 200 to 300 million just to keep up with the next guy." Is this another form of Darwinism, this time in cultural clothing, yet grounded in size, power, and money? Perhaps, but the authors assembled here demonstrate that bigger is not necessarily better, and that millions of dollars do not guarantee either market sensitivity or institutional competence. The reader will also note that reputation, name recognition, and the trust of visitors are not the property of bigness, as worthiness can be achieved by organizations of any size. There is little danger that the spectacular will replace the speculative at the institutions described in this book.

Of particular concern is that many museums now see no other way but to consume their way to survival or prosperity, failing to recognize that this is an outdated economic perspective. This is doubly puzzling in light of the discernment that should accompany the historical legacy of museums as knowledge-based institutions. Nevertheless, most of us remain seduced by the desire for more of everything, and marketplace economics continues to dominate our culture and worldview. This should, however, be a cause for concern among those many museums that have staked their future on attendance figures, earned revenues and culture as entertainment. Recent research indicates that the museum sector is struggling to maintain its audiences, and that the visitor base is declining (Burton & Scott 2003: 56–57). Nor has there been any diversification in the traditional visitor profile, which is still marked by high income and a high level of education. In addition, there is much anecdotal information which suggests that earned revenues are not infinitely expandable, which is further complicated by the complete failure of museum practitioners and funding agencies to thoughtfully consider what constitutes an appropriate balance between public funding, private funding, and earned revenues for public institutions.

Much of this looming crisis, along with the attendant pressures on management, is a result of a widespread misconception in Western society that markets create communities. The opposite, in fact, is true, as the marketplace and its activities actually deplete trust (Rifkin 1997). It is the organizations of the non-profit sector, neither government nor business, which build and enrich the trust, caring, and genuine relationships – the social capital – upon which the marketplace is based. These organizations range from political parties, to museums, to Girl Guides, and there would be no markets without this web of human relationships. Social capital is born of long-term associations that are not explicitly self-interested or coerced, and typically diminishes if it is not regularly renewed or replaced (Bullock & Trombley 1999: 798). The contributors to this book are fully aware of this, and they provide rich case studies in the creation of social capital and its vast potential as a source of meaning and inspiration. What if our political and business leaders realized that business of all kinds can only be properly conducted in a society rich in social capital? This might result in non-profits, including museums, being measured in terms of the *social* capital they generate, and being compensated accordingly. Grants and handouts would become artifacts, and museums would be paid for the value they add to individuals and communities. All of the institutions described here would find themselves in enviable positions in such a world, as they have become highly skilled at creating the trust, empathy and meaning that constitute social capital. Because none of this work is inspired by the marketplace, these organizations also serve to counteract the three thousand marketing messages each of us is now subjected to each day. As Mark Kingwell (1998: 45) notes, none of these messages have anything to do with thinking or knowledge, much less meaning: they are about buying stuff.

The relentless erosion of meaning in everyday life, and its replacement with culture as consumption, goes beyond our alienation from nature and the imperatives of the marketplace. Although not necessarily a cause, the emotional narcissism of the Baby Boomer generation is another factor to consider. It is not this generation's creative intelligence that is at issue, but rather its tendency towards extreme individualism. We introduce this notion here with some apprehension, recognizing that the bulk of current museum leaders in North America are of this generation, as are most of the contributors to this book. Because the influence of this birthright on the organizational behaviour of museums is neither recognized nor debated, it invites speculation. It is important to note that narcissism is not only the overvaluing of self and one's abilities, but is also the undervaluing of others and their contributions. This is a normal trait of childhood and is mostly outgrown with age, although critics argue that the Boomer generation is characterized by a very high cognitive capacity coupled with persistent selfishness (Wilber 2001: 17–32).

In short, this narcissistic individualism can culminate in an inability to take other people, places, and things into account. Determining to what extent this trait can be extended to the contemporary management of museums is dangerous, but one question cannot be ignored: Is the current insularity and fragmentation of the museum community related to the emotional makeup of Baby Boomers, or is it merely a coincidence? There is nearly continuous rhetoric on the need for partnership and collaboration between museums, as well as with their communities, with only modest results to date. If meaning is to be found in the relationship of the individual to community, and the opportunity this provides to find out who one is (McKibben 2003: 18), it is axiomatic that museums have a primary role in facilitating this search. Perhaps only a generational change in leadership will fulfil this promise.

Setting aside any further speculation on the peculiarities of Boomers, there is ample evidence to conclude that they have contributed to the erosion of meaning in another way. It is this generation which has significantly influenced academic studies and continues to "extend an egalitarian embrace to every stance, no matter how shallow or narcissistic," including deconstructive postmodernism (Wilber 2001: 26–28). Postmodernism is the school of thought based on the assumption that an objective evaluation of competing points of view is impossible, since all points of view are to some extent biased by race, gender and culture (Woodhouse 1996: 22). Although such biases are a fact of life and mostly unavoidable, the danger in adopting this postmodern perspective is that we abandon passion and critical thought, both of which are key ingredients in the search for meaning, in the name of relativism. The postmodern result is a mishmash of pluralistic relativism and fragmented pluralism, where everything is of equal weight and value, and everyone does their own thing. Thus emerges the paradoxical individual – empowered and enabled, but also isolated and disconnected (McKibben 2003: 16). Where once the church, the village, and the extended family reconciled this meaninglessness, we are now in need of alternatives.

Apart from postmodernism's contribution to fragmented thinking, it is important to note another inherent danger in this school of thought. Postmodernism has also been called the culture of no resistance, having abandoned the "arrogance" of trying to figure out the origins, logic, causality, and structure of the world we live in (Zernan 2001: 88). Forsaking the effort to understand our shared experience is perilous, especially in light of our relentless materialism. The socially responsible museum is capable of providing a different source of meaning for its community, politely oblivious to the narrow agendas of both the corporatists and the postmodernists.

There is nothing to be gained, however, by retreating from the status quo, as environmental destruction, postmodernism, capitalism, and Boomeritis are embedded in our lives. They have been slowly gathering force and substance, and are now so predominant in our society that they demand a response. These social, environmental and technological pressures have, in effect, created a metaphorical fork in the road, not only for individuals, but also for museums. This fork is an opportunity to choose another path, especially for those who have pondered the outcome of North America's current trajectory.

Many museums have made a choice, knowingly or unknowingly, to pursue popularity and increased revenues through high-profile exhibitions and architectural sensationalism. This strategy is so consumptive of staff and money that there is often little left of either to pursue other activities. Yet many museums are succeeding at this, especially the larger ones, although the long-term sustainability of this business plan is not yet known. Some of these museums have come to resemble corporate entities, even at this early stage, with revenues and attendance being the predominant measures of worth. Many of their boards of directors are also increasingly indistinguishable from their corporate counterparts, with the directors chosen for their business experience, corporate tribalism or ostensible influence in fundraising. Although such qualifications are not new in the arts world, the danger lies in the growing tendency for these boards to self-select on the basis of these criteria, to the exclusion of other attributes reflecting gender, cultural diversity and specialized knowledge unrelated to business.

The museums portrayed in this book have pondered the metaphorical fork in the road and chosen a different path, with a new sensibility. It is important to note, however, that they are also continuing to engage in traditional museum work at the same time. Although embracing a socially responsible mission does not require forsaking either education or entertainment, it does require an intuitive appreciation of certain values that are largely absent or unspoken in contemporary museum work (Block 2002: 47–65). To name or discuss some of these qualities might invite ridicule or embarrassment, as they appear to bear little or no relationship to bottom-line thinking about revenues and expenditures. The truth is actually more complex, and the articles presented here demonstrate that idealism, intimacy, depth, and interconnectedness are not only the warp and weft of meaning, but are also the foundation for long-term sustainability.

The how and the why are to be found in the stories which follow, and all of them consistently illustrate that these four values, far from being New Age hype, are rather the touchstones for creating meaning in a community. Idealism, intimacy, depth, and interconnectedness are the tests of genuineness and quality in a socially responsible museum, in contrast to the current preoccupation with attendance figures. The premise of this book is that attendance flows from significance, and significance flows from the provision of meaning and value to one's community. These are the true faces of sustainability. Blockbuster exhibitions have certainly demonstrated their ability to bring in crowds and revenue, but in ways much like an addictive substance. The impact is fast and undeniable, but quickly dissolves in the quest for more, and there is never enough. One senior museum director, highly successful at profit-making blockbusters, noted that these exhibitions were eroding his museum's brand (Bill Barkley, personal communication, 2001). Many people were only visiting when there was a blockbuster, none of which had anything to do with the museum's unique strengths and abilities.

The museums discussed in this book demonstrate that there are choices to be made which go beyond the role of impresario, if one is willing to grapple with the four values mentioned above. This task must begin with idealism, which means thinking about the way things could be, rather than simply accepting the way things are. All of the contributors to this book are not only preoccupied with this, but they also have a penchant for action. There is little doubt that envisaging an ideal future is not a popularity contest, especially when it becomes the core of your institutional vision. But it is this idealism, this striving for constant improvement in the human condition, which separates the socially responsible from the socially aware.

Idealism does not count for much without intimacy, as intimacy is about communication and the quality of the contact which is made. Quality communication lies in direct experience, so it makes sense that electronic and virtual interaction are only part of the solution. Although they lack quality and intimacy, they do provide broad exposure, which is valuable in its own right. In the end, there is no substitute for human relationships, and all the time, energy, and consideration they require. All the museums discussed in this book have made deep and enduring commitments to the maintenance of human relationships, which in turn have led unavoidably to depth, the third value so critical to the creation of meaning. Depth is about being thorough and complete, even when this requires a tremendous investment of time and resources. You will learn of organizations in this book that have invested decades of staff time in building relationships with particular groups of people, all in an effort to try to understand what is important. Depth is about thinking, questioning and reflecting, and taking the time to do this. Be warned that the obstacles to such a commitment are endemic, beginning with our society's addiction to speed and superficiality in our daily lives. Speed is the antithesis of depth (Block 2002: 51).

Finally, there is the matter of interconnectedness, a word which is sure to send the empirically minded running for the hills. In fact, there is more substance to this notion than one might assume, as there is a growing societal awareness of the interconnectedness of things, including families, organizations, the environment, and the whole of humanity. It is increasingly difficult to deny that our own well-being is indissolubly linked to the health of society and our environment (Leonard & Murphy 1995: xi). Even science is searching for more comprehensive models that are truer to our understanding of the interconnectedness of space and time, and the body and the mind (Kabat-Zinn 1990: 151). It is no longer tenable to ignore the undesirable consequences of our apparently unthinking adherence to marketplace ideology, with its sole emphasis on individual and corporate autonomy. Make no mistake, it is an ideology. It is an integrated set of assumptions, theories and aims that constitute a socio-political program and agenda. Worst of all, it is marked by the truculence of certainty (Whalley 1959: 69).

This book is proof that there are alternatives, and that a sense of interconnectedness is an antidote to the inevitable uncertainty which pervades any attempt to learn and think in new ways. Moreover, making your institution vulnerable, and hence more responsive to your community, is neither a new nor a revolutionary idea. As noted later in this book, John Cotton Dana, the American librarian, believed that museums should grow out of the individual nature of their communities, and that they should be accountable to the public (Grove 1978: 33). Dana advised his contemporaries to "learn what aid the community needs, and fit the museum to those needs." He said this eighty-five years ago.

If the reader is annoyed with or threatened by the idea of moving beyond the museum as temple or forum (Cameron 1971), there is another, more constructive way, to view the work described here. It is also about organizational renewal and all that means for enhancing long-term sustainability, and herein lies the true challenge of intelligent management. In effect, individuals, organizations, and societies start slowly, grow, prosper, and decline (Handy 1994: 49–63). Decline is not inevitable if you are willing to challenge all the assumptions underlying current success, and this must begin with questions, which then lead to ideas. This is paradoxical, because this must be done at a time when all the messages coming through are that everything is just fine. As the articles in this book clearly demonstrate, each organization must find its own way in this process. The critical requirement is to begin the exploration by being skeptical, curious and inventive before you have to be. If you don't do this before you are forced to, chances are that you are already in decline. This work is well underway in the examples presented here, and they provide both guidelines and lessons that might assist those who have an interest in acting on what matters.

To begin with, it is helpful to consider this work as purpose-filled experiments, whose intention is just as much about learning as it is about achieving (Block 2002: 3). In doing so, the choice of a worthy destination is much more important that simply settling for what we know will work. This, in turn, requires a willingness to address questions that have no answers. This is not as daunting or unrealistic as it may sound, recognizing that new knowledge comes when you simply bear in mind what you need to know (Wilber 2001: 39). Put another way, keep holding the problem in mind and it will yield; it is the will and the passion to do this that are most important. Time, patience, and commitment are also essential. You may also expect to feel a bit like an outsider as you confront these responsibilities, as there is good reason to believe that acting on what matters may mean living on the margins of our institutions and culture (Block 2002: 84–85), at least for awhile. Cultivating some detachment from the mainstream may mean lower attendance figures than a blockbuster could provide, or perhaps silence or rude skepticism from one's colleagues, but the museums discussed in this book are proof that these issues eventually become less troublesome.

Such difficulties are to be expected if one is in search of genuine accountability, which is not the easiest sort of accountability, nor the obvious choice, for many museums. The accountability portrayed in this book is about purpose in the workplace, including questions of social responsibility, social equity, civic engagement, and the meaning the institution has for the community (Block 2002: 190). For all those museum practitioners wedded to traditional practices or current formulas of success, we reiterate that this kind of accountability is not mutually exclusive, and can be achieved while getting the other work of the organization done. Most importantly,

> There is nothing lacking. Nothing more is needed than what we already have. We require no remarkable, undiscovered technologies. We do not need heroic, larger-than-life leadership. The only requirement is that we, as individuals, choose a revitalizing future and then work in community with others to bring it to fruition. (Elgin 1993: 193)

If reluctance still lurks in the thought of assuming responsibility without authority, museums must ask themselves from whence they think their authority will come. Because museums will never be in control of society or communities, waiting around for the authority to act responsibly is as heedless as it is impossible. There is no barrier to social responsibility, and no one way to pursue it, as these articles illustrate. Discontent will also be unavoidable – discontent from failed experiments, discontent from the keepers of the status quo, and discontent from never being certain. The contributors to this book know all about this, but they also know it is "better to play the edge of discontent, the inevitable escort of transformation" (Leonard & Murphy 1995: 51).

As the editors, we are obligated to make known our most obvious biases and assumptions as we conclude this introduction. First, we assume that we can be the co-creators of our lives, both personal and professional, if we accept the responsibility to do so. Second, we assume that museums are among the most free and creative work environments on the planet. In contrast to the private sector, they do not have production or sales quotas, nor do they suffer the malaise of creating false needs. Unlike the public sector, museums are not forced to administer unpopular government policies. In short, museums are privileged work environments. How many people in the twenty-first century are able to work in organizations whose purpose is their meaning (Handy 1994: 183)? All museum workers share this privilege.

Last, we assume that learning is essential to the intelligent and caring change that our world requires, and learning requires that we ask difficult, and perhaps rude, questions of ourselves and others. Self-critical thought is rapidly becoming a survival skill, however reluctant the museum establishment is to concede this necessity. Encouraging some serious reflection on the nature of social responsibility in museums is, without question, the main motivation for assembling this volume.

We also believe, as career museum workers, that much lies beyond both the ingrained acquisitiveness of museums and their ever-increasing commitment to entertainment. With respect to the former, we note with dismay the recent "Declaration on the Importance and Value of Universal Museums" (The Arts Business Exchange 2002: 14). In this document, the directors of eighteen of the world's most prominent art museums conceded that calls to repatriate objects that have belonged to museum collections for many years have become an important issue for museums. They also declared that "to narrow the focus of museums whose collections are diverse and multifaceted would therefore be a disservice to all visitors." Cutting through the ambiguity of this statement, it means that repatriation is no longer an issue for the world's most elite cultural institutions, irrespective of the merits of the case. We cannot help but liken this perspective to the aging generals of the First World War, who, having been brought up on horses, simply assumed that the world would remain the same. The consequences of this inertia may be not be as severe for the cultural elite as it was for the troops, but it will be just as humiliating.

As a society, we continue to amuse ourselves to death (Postman 1985), and museums appear to be increasingly compelled to do the same. Whether it is plastic replicas of Egyptian funerary objects, or the mummified remains of our Neolithic ancestors, many museums have joined the perpetual round of entertainments. We understand the short-term economic necessity of seeing people only as audiences, but we also hope that the search for meaning will survive to inspire the next generation of museum workers, perhaps less beholden to the tyranny of the marketplace or undisguised ethnocentrism. There is still inspiration to be had, such as that contained in the following account.

One of the most quoted phrases from the American Indian Wars was Crazy Horse's comment at a battle in which the Lakota were outnumbered. He is regularly quoted as having said, "Today is a good day to die"

14   INTRODUCTION

(Lopez 1978: 5), although no one pays much attention to the second part of his remark. What he actually said was, "Today is a good day to die, for all the things of my life are here." Without presuming any comparison between our world view and that of the First Nations, we would like to think that museums have a role to play in helping to create that continuous sense of a full life that Crazy Horse must have been talking about. Museums are uniquely placed to foster this sense of interrelatedness, along with the deep respect required for inter-cultural understanding, easing the plight of the disadvantaged and stewarding the environment. We would also like to think that museums, as social institutions, might one day become integral to one's perception of life, a life that is both complete and fully at home in the community and in the natural world. This is a choice that any museum can make, and many are already doing so. For the others, we hope this book will help point the way.

WHAT FOLLOWS

The following chapters demonstrate how museums can fulfil their search for meaning by building new kinds of relationships with their publics. The way in which an audience is defined impacts how a museum will develop. Ruth J. Abram is situated in the lower East Side of New York City, and her museum tells the story of the changing occupancy of a tenement in the area. The ongoing hardships of its occupants help neighbourhood residents understand their own situation, while questioning the rest of us about the propriety of such living conditions within the most prosperous of economies. Susan Pointe resuscitated an underutilized art gallery at the University of Alberta Hospital by refocusing the intent of the entire program. She took art out of the gallery space, where few visitors, staff or patients viewed it, and brought it to the wards, using multidisciplinary teams of artists and performers. Janet Pieschel is addressing some of the more difficult issues in our society. The Calgary Police Interpretive Centre (CPIC) brings school children face to face with the consequences of such problems as drunk driving, prostitution, drug abuse, and family violence. In addition to its deterrent message, the CPIC also serves as an avenue through which troubled students can seek help to remove themselves from such situations. At the Glenbow Museum, the Chevron-Texaco Open Minds Program (Michèle Gallant and Gillian Kydd) brings school classes to the museum for an entire week. Students are energized and the museum is transformed from exhibit site to an experimental learning centre.

In our Western society, "science" is often seen to be at once the cause and the panacea for all that ails us (and our planet). It is not surprising, therefore, that science museums are also addressing important questions and finding new ways to involve communities in searching for answers. The Liberty Science Center (Emlyn H. Koster and Stephen H. Baumann) is exemplary in using science to make a difference in the quality of people's lives. Joanne DiCosimo outlines a similar mandate for the Canadian Museum of Nature, one of Canada's federally operated national museums. She is clear that the "national" museums must include the entire nation in their decision-making, or risk becoming irrelevant. Glenn S. Sutter and Douglas Worts provide an excellent example of how such collaborations come to fruition through exhibitions that clarify ecological issues while underscoring the need for personal accountability and responsibility.

Relationships between indigenous peoples and museums have long been overshadowed by our colonial past. Indigenous people often view museums as agents of cultural plunder, and see their collections as culture held hostage. Until recently, the exclusion of alternative voices in museums has reinforced this image. Gerald T. Conaty and Beth Carter relate how the Blackfoot people have become full partners with the Glenbow Museum in the interpretation of their culture. Paul Tapsell describes the removal of Maori skeletal remains to foreign museums and the current repatriation process. These are examples of indigenous peoples who are regaining control of their own destinies, as well as the central role museums can play in this process.

The authors range from scientists and anthropologists to artists and social activists. Hence, some papers are more "academic" while others are less so. Collectively, they represent experiments at redefining what museums can be. It is our hope that others will look at their own communities and themselves, and find new ways of drawing connections and adding value.

ENDNOTES

1   The word "museum" is meant to be inclusive and include all types of museums, art galleries, and science centres.

REFERENCES

Ames, Michael
    1992   De-schooling the museum: a proposal to increase public access to museums and their resources. In *Cannibal tours and glass boxes. The anthropology of museums*, edited by Michael Ames, pp. 88–97. Vancouver: University of British Columbia Press.
The Arts Business Exchange
    2002   Museum directors issue statement on object repatriation. Electronic Newsletter, p. 14. Contact *editor@artsbusiness.com*
Bennett, Tony
    1996   The museum and citizen. In Tony Bennett, Robin Trotter and Donna McAlear (Eds.), *Museums and Citizenship: a resource book. Memoirs of the Queensland Museum, 39*(1).
Block, Peter
    2002   *The answer to how is yes.* San Francisco: Berrett-Koehler.
Brown, Joseph Epes
    1989   *The spiritual legacy of the American Indian.* New York: Crossroad.
Bullock, Alan and Trombley, Stephen (Eds.)
    1999   *The new Fontana dictionary of modern thought.* Hammersmith and London: HarperCollins.
Burton, Christine and Scott., Carol
    2003   Museums: Challenges for the 21st century. *International Journal of Arts Management, 5*(2): 56–68.
Cameron, Duncan F.
    1971   The museum, a temple or the forum. *Curator, 14*(1), 11–24.
Elgin, Duane
    1993   *Voluntary simplicity.* Revised Edition (First Edition 1981). New York: Quill, William Morrow.
Grasset, Constance D.
    1996   Museum fever in France. *Curator, 39*(3), 188–207.
Grove, Richard
    1978   John Cotton Dana. *Museum News* (May/June), 33–39, 86–88.
Handy, Charles
    1994   *The age of paradox.* Boston: Harvard Business School Press.
Hume, Christopher
    2000   Arts story: Cultural vacuum. *The Toronto Star* (August 26), 1–5 (taken from thestar.com).
Kabat-Zinn, Jon
    1990   *Full catastrophe living.* New York: Delta Trade Paperbacks, Bantam, Doubleday, Dell.
Kingwell, Mark
    1998   Fast forward. *Harper's, 296* (1776; May), 37–46.

Leonard, George and Murphy, Michael
    1995   *The life we are given*. New York: G.P. Putnam's Sons.
Lopez, Barry (Ed.)
    1978   The American Indian mind. *Potentials, Quest* /78, 1–16.
McKibben, Bill
    2003   The posthuman condition. *Harper's, 396* (1835; April), 15–19.
Postman, Neil
    1985   *Amusing ourselves to death*. New York: Penguin.
Rifkin, Jeremy
    1997   The end of work. Address on behalf of the Volunteer Centre of Calgary (November 13, 1997). Palliser Hotel, Calgary, Alberta, Canada.
Whalley, George
    1959   Address to the graduating class. *The Blue and White*, Rothesay College School, New Brunswick, (pp. 64–71).
Wilber, Ken
    2001   *A theory of everything*. Boston: Shambhala.
Woodhouse, Mark B.
    1996   *Paradigm wars*. Berkeley: Frog.
Zerzan, John
    2001   Greasing the rails to a cyborg future. *Adbusters* (May/June), *35*, 88.

HISTORY IS AS HISTORY DOES: THE EVOLUTION OF A MISSION-DRIVEN MUSEUM

Ruth J. Abram

AN IDEA TAKES SHAPE

Perhaps like mine, your mother used to say, "Handsome is as handsome does." To my southern belle mother, to whom looks count quite a bit, actions nevertheless count more – much more. I agree with my mother, and I believe that it is as true of institutions as it is of human beings. What institutions *do*, rather than what they say, what they own, or the nature of their physical edifice reflects *who* they are and, therefore, whether they are of consequence.

Had anyone looked closely when the Lower East Side Tenement Museum opened for business in 1988 (and few did), s/he would have understood that the museum intended to offer history as a resource for shaping the future. It was clear from its mission statement: "To promote tolerance and historic perspective through the presentation and interpretation of the variety of immigrant and migrant experiences on Manhattan's Lower East Side, a gateway to America."

What was not clear – to anyone – was just how it would do this. But it has become increasingly clear, as the museum has insisted on asking not only *What is the history?* but also *What can the history do ... to improve the world?*

Indeed, the very idea for the Tenement Museum grew not from any interest (or knowledge) in historic preservation, but rather from my experience as an activist. A question common to all the work I had previously done – in organizations working on behalf of racial and gender equality and civil liberties – was: *How will we be one nation and at the same time appreciate, enjoy, or at least not be threatened by the often profound differences we bring to the table based on our backgrounds?* The other underlying issue was: *How will we create a truly equitable society, where we stop using gender, race, class, or other factors as excuses to treat a group of people less well and to deny them equal opportunity?*

Could a history museum prompt visitors to ask these questions? Could it interest them in finding solutions to these and related, enduring social issues? Could it accomplish these things while creating a neutral ground for dialogue?

In my earlier work, I had been distressed by the apparent acceptance by some of the leaders of my organizations that our message – whether civil liberties, civil rights, or women's rights – had limited appeal. They assumed that the general public would automatically reject the message out of ignorance, or fear, or both. Feminist leaders cautioned me to eschew any involvement with corporate women, lest they corrupt "our" message. Similarly, closet feminists who staffed organizations of women they regarded as conservative, insisted that their constituents would *never* respond to the fundamental principles espoused by the feminist movement of the 1970s. Like the leaders of so many other causes, these feminists opted to "hunker down" with the converted few, rather than risk the anticipated rejection of women whom they had designated as the Other. Rejecting this point of view, I made a point of obtaining speaking engagements before audiences ranging from corporate women to women from the heart of America's Bible Belt, and was rewarded by an eager response. Along the way, I learned that in order to be heard, I had to find a way to relate to my audiences' particular concerns, and to do so in a language with which they were comfortable. In other words, I had to be respectful.

I brought the lessons of my movement work to the Tenement Museum. Paramount among them was the belief that to realize its mission, the museum's programming had to be predicated on the idea that everyone could learn, and that everyone would be welcomed and engaged, regardless of background, in that learning process. The museum would have to afford every visitor a safe place in which to contemplate his or her opinions about the issues presented. Simply put, to prosper the museum had to respect the public – *all* the public.

From my social work training I knew that diverse people, who regard themselves as different from one another, are more likely to unite if they can find common ground. Most Americans are descendants of people who came, willingly or not, from somewhere else. We share family histories containing the immigrant and migrant experiences of dislocation, relocation, and reinvention. Deciding to build on this common experience, I introduced long-rooted Americans to their family members – at the point of their arrival, when they knew not the language, the accent, or the customs of their adopted land and before they were economically secure. I hoped that, by connecting with revered ancestors, Americans would be moved to participate in a national conversation with similarly situated, contemporary immigrants and other "outsiders." Further, I hoped that Americans might realize that contemporary "strangers" have much in common with the forebears they so admire. For those newly arrived or struggling, I hoped to offer the comfort that comes from the knowledge that, as immigrants or migrants, they were part of a vital American tradition; and that others – many others – had experienced and often overcome the same challenges facing them.

With the critical assistance of Anita Jacobson, who now serves as a trustee of the museum, I launched the Tenement Museum out of a twelve-foot by sixty-eight-foot storefront, previously occupied by a shoe shop, in the basement of 97 Orchard Street. It took five years to convince the owner to sell the tenement property.

Rejecting the rather compelling idea of using the building as a stage set for the stories of all the area's history and people, we decided to capitalize on the power of place by limiting the interpretation inside our tenement to the stories of the people actually associated with the property – as owners, shopkeepers and tenants from 1863 to 1935. Once the tenement building was secured, research began on these "alumni." Using census, voting, marriage, death, military, religious and other records, researchers identified over thirteen hundred names.

Believing that to engage and challenge the public we needed to reach their hearts, we decided to select dramatic stories, and to give the stories pride of place. That meant the artifacts would be supportive of the stories, not the other way around. We also wanted stories that together expressed the change over time in the history of the building's population, from English, Irish, and German Protestants and Catholics, to German Jews, Eastern European Jews, Sephardic Jews, and Sicilian Catholics, with considerable overlap. We looked for stories that had clear relevance to contemporary society. It turned out there were plenty from which to choose: a woman whose husband disappeared, a family forced onto relief rolls, a sweatshop worker who succumbed to tuberculosis, and a family stung by prejudice never experienced in their homeland. The overarching theme common to all these stories was, of course, immigration, and America's changing views about it.

THE LOWER EAST SIDE TENEMENT MUSEUM

The core visitor experience at the Tenement Museum is a guided tour of a nineteenth-century tenement building. Erected by a German-born tailor in 1863, this six-story, brick structure occupies a lot twenty-five feet wide by eighty-eight feet deep. There are four 325-square-foot apartments per floor. Originally constructed without indoor plumbing, ventilation, or light, it was nevertheless sufficient for the owner and his family, who moved right in. Before its condemnation as a residence in 1935, the building was home to an estimated total of seven thousand immigrants from over twenty nations.

Although more citizens trace the beginning of their families' American experience to the urban rather than the rural environment, and most descend from working-class immigrants, 97 Orchard Street is the first homestead of urban working-class and poor immigrant people to be preserved and interpreted in the United States. This, in itself, serves as a corrective in the landscape of historic sites, which have heretofore utterly failed to explore this now majority aspect of our national heritage.

Today, five carefully restored apartments set the stage on which guides introduce visitors to immigrant families who actually lived in 97 Orchard Street. In the Museum's *Getting By* tour, visitors meet the Gumpertz and Baldizzi families struggling against the ravages of the great economic depressions of the 1870s and 1930s, respectively. German-born Natalie Gumpertz is the first female household head ever presented in a National Historic Site. Similarly, through the Sicilian Baldizzi family, visitors meet illegal immigrants and explore the issue of private and public welfare and the questions that endure: Whom should society help? To what extent? On what basis?

In the *Piecing It Together* tour, visitors consider New York's garment industry – past and present. Looking at two Jewish families, in the 1880s and again at the turn of the century, visitors see the industry move from home-based "sweatshops" to factory operations. In the Levine garment shop, just a few feet away from the humming sewing machines and the steam of the presser's heavy irons, Jennie Levine gives birth to her third child, assisted by an immigrant midwife. (Jennie's fifth delivery will be in a hospital – the American way.) Entering the Rogarshevsky home in 1918, set at the moment the family is *sitting shiva* (observing the Jewish tradition of seven days of mourning), visitors come face-to-face with death itself and with the ever-present tendency to blame the victims of an epidemic. Tuberculosis, which claimed the life of the family's patriarch, Abraham, a presser in a garment factory, was then referred to as the *Jewish Disease*, yet proportionately fewer Jews had it than did members of other groups.

The stories are full of difficulties but, like our own stories, are not without their triumphs. Thus, museum docents explain not only that Natalie Gumpertz's shoemaker husband disappeared, but also that she established a dress-making business that was sufficient to build a foundation for her family's success in America. The Baldizzi apartment is interpreted on the day they were evicted, but visitors cannot miss the morning glories, planted by Mr. Baldizzi in a cheese box supplied by government relief, which spiral up the window. Years later, his daughter, Josephine, recalled the effectiveness of her father's strategies for warding off despair: "To this day, mention the Great Depression, and my first thought is morning glories."

By presenting three-dimensional stories of people who experience depression and delight, tragedy and triumph, we hope to offer our tenement's characters as historical role models. Because our lives are also multi-dimensional and complex, whether we are rich or poor, formally educated or illiterate, we can relate to 97 Orchard Street's people and learn from them.

Docent-led Tours

Fire regulations and our desire to make visitors feel welcome prompted us to make our tours docent-led. There are no ropes, no text labels, and no glass cases in the historic immigrant apartments. Docents help preserve the historic fabric, convey the family stories, and interact with visitors. Thirty-two full-time staff and thirty part-time docents make up the museum's guide staff. Tour groups of fifteen people start every twenty minutes, seven days a week. Quality control is the obvious challenge, and as the museum has grown, so too has the process of training and evaluating tour guides. At this writing, we are overhauling the training program to further emphasize the importance of good storytelling, interaction with visitors, and inviting visitors' questions and stories. We are also instituting a more formal evaluation process. The relatively few visitor complaints about a tour guide have been met with an automatic apology and a refund. It is obviously in the museum's interest to make every tour a rewarding experience. Many have questioned the efficacy of our approach. Certainly it is expensive (though having all full-time staff conduct tours cuts down on some of the cost), and it is time consuming to train staff. But the result is a rare combination of intellectual and emotional experience for visitors, which makes the effort worthwhile.

Americans Want to Learn From Their Encounters With History

In the first survey of Americans' relationship to history, conducted in 1999, Roy Rosenzweig and David Thelen found that "Americans feel at home with the past; day to day; hour to hour, the past is present in their lives" (Rosenzweig & Thelen 1998: 36). In addition, "Americans ... want to make a difference, to take responsibility for themselves and others. And so, they assemble their experiences into patterns, narratives that allow them to make sense of the past, set priorities, project what might happen next and try to shape the future" (p. 12). In other words, Americans regard the past as a usable tool. So do I.

The question is how to make the past available in such a way that it can be easily used to this end.

THE USE OF HISTORY

Last year, a management expert asked the full-time staff if anyone could state the museum's mission. To his utter amazement, twenty-five voices rose in unison to recite the museum's mission statement by heart. From its inception, the mission has been central to the museum's work. All of our programs and policies are measured against their capacity to advance it. I have come to believe that more than anything else, the museum's success in communicating its mission and its sustained efforts to advance it both internally and externally account for its ability to attract, retain and motivate an exceptionally fine staff.

Liz Sevcenko, vice president for programs, oversees the design and implementation of the museum's public programs. Liz explained:

> Being the American-born child of an immigrant father with multiple identities was, for me, a defining experience. My Dad would frequently respond to something I said or did by asking, "Are you an American?" In this way and in others, he constantly reminded me that behaviour I considered normal, was not necessarily normal in another society. This perspective was an uncomfortable one for a kid, but it inspired me to look at my own world – not just to accept it. Then too, my academic parents traveled a lot. Before we visited some person they knew in the foreign country, my mother would tell me what to expect and how to act in accordance with their customs. In time, I found I was most comfortable in situations where I was obviously different, and I looked for them.

In her college history classes Liz discovered "that things I thought fixed and permanent in the world, were not. I saw that often they'd been some other way before, and that individual people had and could again make change. I learned that race and gender were historically defined, and that depending on the time, the same person could be classified differently. I came to feel that the historical perspective could be the most powerful tool for social change."

With her sensitive antennae for differences, her preference for situations where those differences exist and are acknowledged, and her belief in the power of history, Liz had the right credentials for the hard task of inserting the concept of the *usable past* into all the museum's programs.

Learning that area immigrants were waiting up to three years for places in free English classes, the museum initiated its own, with a curriculum that incorporated the diaries, letters and memoirs of earlier immigrants. "I not only learned English," declared a graduate, "I learned I was not alone." Upon discovering that nineteenth-century immigrants were often met at Ellis Island by charity workers who provided employment or housing advice, a student exclaimed, "No one was there for us at Kennedy Airport!" With that, the idea for an immigrant resource guide was conceived. The first edition, developed in collaboration with the New York Times Company and published in Chinese, Spanish and English, contains stories of immigrants past and present, a list of immigrant-assisting organizations, and answers to the most commonly asked questions. It was the history of immigration that furnished the newest arrivals with a fresh sense of possibility and emboldened them to act.

Teaming up with private and public schools, the museum developed a program with a simple message: *a person's worth cannot be measured by calculating his/her material wealth*. As a first step, nine-year-olds were invited to write down words they associated with the word "poor" both before and after a visit to the Tenement Museum. The number of negative associations with the word "poor" (including *mean, dangerous, dishonest*) plummeted from ninety before the visit to twenty after it. The resulting program, *Networth*, has been piloted with Lyndhurst, a property of the National Trust for Historic Preservation, and the Frick Museum in New York City.

Well aware that many of the some thirty thousand school children who visit the museum annually return to homes that are less adequate than the museum's nineteenth-century tenement – or to no homes at all – the museum developed a program to teach the history of immigration, housing and nineteenth-century reform, as well as citizenship and advocacy skills. In cooperation with the city's Department of Housing and Preservation, the museum trains children to recognize violations of the early twentieth-century housing codes at the museum's tenement. Returning home, the children check their own housing and report violations to the appropriate authority.

INFUSING THE CORE VISITOR EXPERIENCE

Through these projects, the museum put *promoting tolerance and historical perspective* into practice. However, the more difficult challenge of infusing the museum's core visitor experience with the *usable past* concept still loomed before us.

The museum's newest apartment, the Levine Garment Shop, gave us the opportunity we needed. Built on two years of scholarship regarding the garment industry past and present, and supported by a Rockefeller Humanities Institute grant, the apartment interprets the story of Jennie and Harris Levine, who came from Poland in 1890 and established a sweatshop in their apartment. Factory inspector records noted that the Levines, who hired non-family members and children for sixty-hour-plus workweeks, were in compliance with the law.

From the beginning, we sought to help visitors use the Levine story as a basis for considering the present situation. What has changed? What has not? To that end, we invited representatives from all sectors of the garment industry – workers, union organizers, manufacturers, designers, government inspectors, and retailers – to participate in the planning. Steve Long, the museum's chief curator, and Pamela Keech, a consulting curator, developed the furnishing plan. "To my way of thinking," said Steve, "objects don't have any intrinsic value. What's important is the meaning and stories we impose upon them. Take the crib in the Levine apartment. It's just an ordinary old crib. But visitors are enthralled by it. Likely it slept both the two- and five-year-old Levine children. With its high sides and placement near the stove, it was the safest and warmest place. Still, it speaks reams about the family's limited choices. Sandwiched between the shop presser, with his hot steaming irons, and the finisher, who is handing the presser the clothes right above the babies' heads, the crib gets people thinking about the Levines and the situation they faced in a new way. When a group of garment workers visited, they said, 'You know, people are always saying garment workers are stupid for taking their children to the factory. But what choice did the Levines have? They needed to keep a close eye on their children, and the best place, despite its dangers, was with them.'"

Because in his own life, Steve routinely uses history to situate himself, the museum's insistence upon using history as a tool for contemporary life seemed natural. "My first question about most any new situation in which I find myself," Steve offered, "is: What's the history? By answering that, I surround myself with others who have been in this situation before and have dealt with similar issues before. In other words, it makes me feel I am not alone." Steve's father has used the Long family history in a similar way. Steve explained, "My great great grandfather, Benjamin Long, built churches and towns in Alabama and founded a coal mine." Steve notes those accomplishments but is more impressed by his great grandfather's maverick political thinking. The next generation was not so successful, and failed to recover from arson and theft. It took the third generation to resuscitate the family; Steve's grandfather became a minister. "But he was quite studious and socially uncomfortable," explained Steve. In his own family, Steve saw that history could inform us about what we *do* and *do not* want to be and do. In this most personal of ways, history was a usable tool for the present.

The Levine tour begins with a taped recording of comments of people working in various segments of the garment industry today. A survey of visitors discovered that the resulting exhibit did indeed stimulate visitors to make comparisons between past and present. We were on our way.

Meanwhile, members of the museum's program team established ten criteria for evaluating all programs, including:

- showcase and interpret the cultural and artistic expressions of immigrants/migrants, past and present;
- raise awareness of the contemporary implications and/or counterparts of the history the museum interprets and offer visitors the means to evaluate these issues on their own;
- stimulate dialogue among people of diverse backgrounds focusing on immigration and related enduring social issues and challenging prejudices based on ethnicity, nationality, class, and race and suggest opportunities for audiences to become involved in addressing these issues;
- encourage and assist immigrants/migrants of all ages to participate fully in political, civic, and social life; collaborate with other Lower East Side community organizations, artists, and residents by integrating reflection on the past into their work.

Examination of all the museum's programs against these criteria clarified the necessity of making other changes. First, we needed to start the visitor experience in a new way. The History Channel came to the rescue, working with the museum staff to produce a film which examined how successive waves of immigrants have struggled in the context of America's ongoing debate as to who and what is American.

We also needed to reconfigure the museum's tours, making more explicit the issues we hoped visitors would recognize as still unresolved.

Cognizant of the powerful, positive impact the history of immigration has on contemporary immigrants, and seeing a benefit to staying current with the contemporary form of the historic story we tell, we determined to make a special effort to reach this audience on a sustained and systematic basis. We established an Immigrant Programs Department, the first in any historic site in the United States. The program's bilingual director, Maggie Russell-Ciardi, now oversees the *Immigrant Art Project*, which brings immigrant visual, dramatic, and digital artists and poets to the museum to produce new work – often in their first languages – about contemporary immigrant experiences. The department also runs a program for immigrants learning English, which features a series of visits to the museum's historic apartments, followed by discussions comparing the immigrant experience past and present as well as information immigrants need about housing, health care, education, and more.

THE MISSION NEEDS TO BE EXPRESSED IN EVERY ASPECT OF THE MUSEUM

It is not productive to place the entire burden for realizing the museum's mission on the program side of the operation. Rather, every department of the museum needs to participate. Senior Vice President Renee Epps, who is responsible for administering the staff as well as the museum's restoration and renovation projects, understands this well. The daughter of parents who both worked in public health and welfare agencies, Renee recalled the conversations that shaped their home. "My Dad talked about his horror over the segregated swimming pools in the Kansas of his youth. My mother spoke movingly of her clients, whether they were teachers or prostitutes." As a child of a family that moved every other year until she was fourteen, Renee had more than her fair share of adjustments to make. She explained, "My experience of being the new kid on the block over and over made me very sensitive to how I was treated. I was grateful to anyone of the kids who befriended me. Often they were poor or of a different age. I realized what mattered is that they wanted to be my friend. My parents encouraged me to accept people for who they were, rather than for any attribute unrelated to character." Renee has brought the lessons of her childhood to bear on the museum community.

Believing that history is as important as health care, the Tenement Museum provides employee coverage in both. All members of the museum's full-time staff, regardless of education, prior training or position, are an integral part of the teaching and learning process. *All* conduct public tours of the museum's land-marked tenement. *All* participate in a weekly program, which includes field trips to area organizations and historical or skills training. *All* participate actively in planning the museum goals and objectives. The topic for each year-long study program is chosen to support a new program; topics have included the history of Chinatown, American immigration, the history of the garment industry, and the history of social welfare and its relationship to immigrants past and present.

The dividends of this investment are great, not only for the staff, but for the museum. As Renee points out, "With every one of the staff conducting public tours, everyone knows why they are working here: it's to serve the public. If you never see the public, you can easily forget." Then, too, because the public really likes the tours, every staff person gets a weekly dose of public praise and appreciation. "Giving my tour is a high point of my week," said Georgina Acevedo, the museum's financial and administrative manager. Born in Puerto Rico, Georgina delights visitors with her own immigrant experience in the course of her tour.

There are additional advantages. Because they are deeply knowledgeable about the history the museum interprets and about its mission and goals, many staff are equipped to represent the museum to the public, to various specialized forums and to the press; and they do. This affords the museum a far greater reach than enjoyed by more traditionally hierarchical institutions.

Many new staff comment on how collegial the atmosphere is. While each person seems quite clear about his or her specific responsibilities, they are quick to assist a colleague. Renee's respect for all types of work is undoubtedly a factor. "I can't stand the 'it's not my job' attitude," she said. "All work is necessary to make the whole thing go. It's unacceptable to denigrate anyone's job by suggesting you are somehow above doing it."

It is obvious that by restoring and interpreting a tenement building, we advance the museum's mission. Less obvious is that the philosophy defining the manner in which the restoration of 97 Orchard Street has been handled is also mission-driven. "Our project is a combination of preservation, conservation, re-creation, and renovation," explained Renee. "We've taken a layered approach. In any given space, you can see all the layers. In this way, we assert that all the years and layers are valid. We're not making decisions for visitors – for instance, about which year is the *most* important. Tolerance includes allowing people to draw their own conclusions."

The museum recently acquired an additional tenement building at 91 Orchard Street to house its offices, archives, conference rooms, and storage. The upper four floors will continue to accommodate primarily immigrant tenants in rent-stabilized and rent-controlled apartments. To allay any fears on the part of the tenants as to the intentions of its new landlord, the museum invited them to a reception. Invitations were issued in English, Chinese, and Spanish. When they arrived, the tenants were told about the museum's plans and they were given a tour of 97 Orchard Street, in whatever language they spoke. Then we began construction, focusing first on correcting decade old electrical and plumbing problems. A letter to Renee from the daughter of one of our tenants attests to the impact of following Renee's management rule – "I ask myself how would I like to be treated in the same circumstance."

> My father … came to this country with nothing but his personal belongings [and moved] into 91 Orchard Street almost 30 years ago. Like most immigrants who did not speak any English, my father worked as a chef and my mother as a seamstress. To provide for [our] family [my parents] have lived very frugally. We are grateful that we have [had] a roof over our heads. Yet for years, my family struggled with past landlords about heat, hot water, and basic repairs. When the bathroom, living room, and bedroom ceilings collapsed, the landlords showed no concern. We had no choice but to complete the repairs ourselves. I am very impressed with the compassion and understanding that you and your staff have shown to my family. My parents would like to thank Peter [Tran] for translating for them, Georgia [Acevedo] for coordinating the rent transfer, and you for answering all their questions and concerns. After so many years of struggles and frustration, my family is happy to be heard.

As Renee says, "The tenants at 91 Orchard Street *are* the present; they are our living example of what has and has not changed about the urban immigrant experience."

EXPANDING THE CONCEPT OF DIVERSITY

Today, it is impossible to attend a museum conference that does not include at least one panel on "diversity," at which panelists discuss how their institutions have sought (often unsuccessfully) to fill one or more positions or board slots with a person of colour. While there is a general agreement that diversity is good, there is not a general understanding that it can take many forms or that it is *absolutely necessary* to the future of museums.

At the Tenement Museum, we believe that *only* if we achieve organization-wide diversity will we realize our institutional goals and objectives. For instance, only because we have staff fluent in Cantonese, Mandarin, and Spanish have we been able to make important contacts with the many neighbourhood people who are fluent in those languages, but not English. Only because we have staff fluent in these languages, as well as in Vietnamese, German, Russian, Italian, and French, are we able to serve thousands of foreign tourists. Our study of the history of the garment industry was greatly enhanced by information from staff members who have worked in it. Similarly, our study of the welfare system was deepened and expanded by the perspectives shared by former recipients on our staff. Finally, each staff member brings his or her special network. The more diverse the staff, the more diverse the network to which the museum has access.

While the museum's success in diversifying staff in positions not requiring museum experience has been excellent, the most senior staff are people from European origins. This is in large measure because the children of America's working class, minority, and immigrant families are not selecting museum work as a profession. The young Asian-American woman who confided in me that her immigrant parents would not hear of her following her passion for art is not an isolated case. Imagining years of struggle and financial insecurity before her, and consequently before them, her parents urged her to take up work in the more secure areas of computers or science, business, or law. Anything except art and museums. The woman is now a banker.

We could have thrown up our hands at the situation, but we did not. Instead, supported by the Chancellor of the City University of New York, the museum collaborated with the university to found the Urban Museum Studies Program. This M.A.–granting program is the first to train the children of working class, minority, and immigrant parents to read and to interpret the urban environment. Absent a plethora of candidates from which to choose, we are trying to grow our own. This is not an overnight process; but the investment is surely worth it.

Because of its location on the edge of New York's Chinatown, the museum felt it was imperative to form relationships with Chinese-American organizations, press, and leaders. That prompted us to seek trustees with connections to this community. The three Chinese-American trustees (a union leader, an accountant with his own firm in Chinatown, and the former director of the Mayor's Office on Immigrant Affairs) who currently serve have been key to the success of the museum's relationship with the area's foreign-born community. The relationship has resulted in press coverage (there are nineteen Asian-language newspapers in New York City), community support, new visitors, and new sources of financial support. One of our trustees has raised thousands of dollars from small businesses in New York's Chinatown. Beyond that, it has proved extremely useful for the museum to have trustees with contacts with the city's various ethnic, religious, and professional networks. For instance, Irish-Americans have helped the museum identify leadership for fundraising for its Irish Family Apartment. The labour leaders on the board helped the museum locate retired garment-shop workers and organizers to be trained as museum docents – the better to draw connections between past and present. And they opened up new funding streams for the museum, making its case to the labour movement.

Another big topic in museum circles is reaching underserved and non-traditional museum audiences. At the Tenement Museum, we have taken that to mean people who have had little experience with museums and therefore don't have them on their entertainment "must see" list, and people who have had disappointing museum experiences. It means people who can't speak the language in which the museum programs, people who can't spare the money for the admission price, or people who have a physical or mental disability.

To reach out to visitors for whom the ticket price is daunting, the museum instituted a good-neighbour program, which annually provides free tickets to hundreds of its already discounted group visitors, and half-price tickets to the third of our visitors who are students. Participants in many special programs come for free as well. To welcome non-English speakers, the museum recruited staff who could conduct group tours in German, French, Spanish, Mandarin, Cantonese, and Russian. Further, it initiated a regularly scheduled Spanish-language tour, and provides pre-booked tours in over five languages. At this writing – six months after launching the Spanish-language tour, and in spite of a barrage of press coverage in English- and Spanish-speaking media, as well as targeted outreach – the response has been poor. Certain there is a market, the museum decided to try new tactics to reach it. A well-publicized tour for Latino leaders and celebrities is in the planning stage.

Although the small dimensions of 97 Orchard Street's hallways and rooms preclude opening this historic site to visitors in wheelchairs, the museum has aggressively sought to serve visitors with other disabilities. An advisory board of disability experts meets regularly. Staff has been instructed in how to serve these visitors. The museum's touch and sign-language tours are popular. Visitors unable to climb our stairs can take a guided photo-tour in our Visitor's Center, or a virtual tour on the web. The large-print materials and assisted-listening devices have made the programs accessible to many visitors who would otherwise be effectively barred from the experience. In a nation in which one in five people has some kind of disability and one in ten has a severe disability, this audience represents a large, mainly untapped and very welcome pool of visitors.

MARKETING, PUBLIC RELATIONS, AND FUNDRAISING MUST SUPPORT THE MISSION

It turns out that the museum's mission not only helps attract and sustain excellent staff and a committed board, it also gives the museum a certain edge with the press. "In every conversation with journalists," explained Katherine Snider, "we lead with the museum's mission. We talk about how much the past and present immigrant stories have in common – especially in a city which is forty percent foreign-born. It differentiates us from other institutions." An immigrant from Montreal, Katherine attributes her early love of history and diversity to her father. "We were a family of mutts – Irish Catholic, Protestant, German Jewish, Lutheran, Catholic, and Anglo-Saxon Protestant. As a boy, my Dad's decidedly un-Irish name forced an outsider status upon him in his parochial Boston Irish Catholic neighbourhood. Montreal, with its incredible diversity, was wonderful for him. He loved the fact that our friends were so diverse and that when we described them, we simply referred to them as friends and did not characterize them by their race or ethnicity as they had in Dad's childhood neighbourhood." Katherine's paternal grandfather had set the stage for this family's tolerance, electing to sit at the Black counter in a segregated Washington, D.C. restaurant in the 1940s. "He thought it [racial segregation] was ridiculous," explained Katherine. Careful to imbue their daughter with their values, the Sniders screened schools for diversity and selected "… a Catholic girls school," recalled Katherine, "whose director was a nun who had converted and was determined to promote tolerance. She established a kosher section of the cafeteria. At every assembly, she spoke on women's rights. Then, too, my family attended an unusual church. When I was eight, the Pope ruled that girls could no longer be altar girls. Our priest would not go along. When I was twelve, the Pope visited our Church. Altar girls participated in the service".

The museum's mission is an expression of staff's internal codes. "I can't imagine," Katherine told me, "ever again working in a place which is not mission-driven. Otherwise, you have to separate your 'real' self and feelings from your work self. Here, there is a seamless relationship between my personal and professional goals." Britta Graf, executive associate to my office, agreed. In the 1970s and '80s, Britta's native Switzerland was alive with agitation for women's rights, civil rights, and a new discussion of immigration and internationalism. "My generation felt compelled to not just go along. We felt we could change the world." But while new to her generation, such feelings were not new for Britta's family. "My grandmother was an ardent pacifist who urged my brother to go to jail rather than to serve in the army." After finishing university and working in women's rights, the AIDS campaign, and a local immigrant project, Britta immigrated to New York City. From many other options, she selected the Tenement Museum, because, "I prefer to work in places which advance my point of view." Britta's abiding interest in, and respect for, people from all walks of life guarantees that people interacting with my office – whether an ambassador, philanthropist, scholar, student, or welfare recipient – will be treated with equal courtesy and dignity. That's a great asset for any institution; it is essential for ours.

There is an inextricable connection between program, public relations, and marketing in a mission-driven institution. "Thanks to members of the Lower East Side Community Preservation Project," explained Katherine, referring to a coalition of over thirty community groups that the museum organized several years ago, "we have met new constituencies and new press." Florence Li, the director of the Chinese American Planning Council, is just one member who has brought many groups in her network to the museum; and before we had the in-house capability, Ms. Li translated our press releases into Chinese. "Of course," Katherine Snider pointed out, "the Chinese-language newspaper staff can speak and read English, but it's a sign of respect to send our release in their first language." Today, reservations for the museum's tour can be made in Spanish; the website features multi-lingual sections, and text for art installations is routinely printed in Spanish, Chinese, and English.

MOVING HISTORY FROM THE PERIPHERY TO THE CENTRE

In spite of the importance "ordinary" Americans have been found to attach to the past, there persists among many activists and opinion leaders the feeling I too once shared: that history is of little practical value to their work. A housing activist invited to speak to the museum staff described her organization's effort to obtain decent housing for economically disadvantaged people, and announced that she could not imagine how the museum could be helpful. Indeed, she charged that by placing issues such as housing and economic inequities in the past, the Tenement Museum could contribute to the problem. If we are to be successful, we need to find convincing ways to respond to this skepticism about history's value. It is worth trying, for as long as history is viewed as an instrument of private but not public value, it will not be afforded a central role in public life. World leaders will continue to form cabinets and other advisory councils with no reference to history. Commissions will be established to grapple with important social policies without regard to historical precedents. Decisions about our future will be made in the absence of understanding the past. This is why the Tenement Museum, indeed any historic site or museum, simply must respond to those who see no practical use for our work.

FINDING PARTNERS FOR A NEW CONCEPT OF HISTORIC SITES

In the Tenement Museum's first decade, I was often frustrated by the lack of acceptance of the principal ideas behind it. Fundraising was unusually difficult; with over twenty years of fundraising experience, I realized that this was more daunting than previous projects. Foundations accustomed to funding traditional museums were uncomfortable with our lack of fine furnishings and art. (I couldn't bring myself to tell them our collection included a rat – an unavoidable part of tenement life.) Before turning us down, one confused foundation official said, "You're not really a museum; you're a settlement house, right?" Foundations that funded social services and/or advocacy routinely returned our proposals unopened, saying, "We don't fund museums." Unaware of the role history plays in the lives of individual Americans, these foundation executives could not imagine that a museum could offer anything to their effort to rectify the world's injustices.

Leaders in preservation derided the idea of including a tenement in the National Register, saying tenements had no redeeming architectural features; there were thousands of them; and that no one of any importance had ever lived in ours. I was dismayed by colleagues in the museum community who described their institutions in terms of square footage rather than mission, and who insisted that the conservative perspectives of their trustees and the perceived tastes and interests of their audiences were insurmountable obstacles to adopting any of the ideas or practices the Tenement Museum espoused.

Feeling isolated and in need of other museum professionals who shared my vision, I went to see the president of a leading foundation. After listening to my concept for the museum and of the difficulties I was experiencing in fundraising, the philanthropist said that the concept was so new that it was difficult for foundations to categorize and therefore easiest just to turn us down. She suggested I look to see if I could find even a handful of directors of historic sites who saw their role as I did.

My letter asking who saw history as I did was answered by directors of eight institutions: the Workhouse (England), the Gulag Museum (Russia), the Slave House (Senegal), The District Six Museum (South Africa), Memoria Abierta (Argentina), the Liberation War Museum (Bangladesh), Terezin Memorial (Czech Republic), and the National Park Service, which presented the Women's Rights National Historical Park and Manzanar (the Japanese internment camp).

Supported by the Rockefeller and Ford foundations and the Trust for Mutual Understanding, these directors travelled to the Rockefeller conference centre in Bellagio, Italy. As we introduced ourselves for the first time, we were amazed to learn that with few exceptions, we had not come from the museum profession to our task. Rather, we shared histories of social activism – against dictatorships and terrorism, against war and poverty, for women's rights and civil rights, as well as other issues. We were activists who had come to believe that our best contribution to the ideas we held dear could be made through history, and specifically, through historic sites. We accepted our roles as formers of public conscience.

After a week of intense discussion, we issued the following statement:

> We are historic site museums in many different parts of the world, at many stages of development, presenting and interpreting a wide variety of historic issues, events and people. We hold in common the belief that it is the obligation of historic sites to assist the public in drawing connections between the history of our sites and its contemporary implications. We view stimulating dialogue on pressing social issues and promoting humanitarian and democratic values as a primary function. To advance this concept, we have formed an International Coalition of Historic Site Museums of Conscience to work with one another.

Our second meeting, again at Bellagio, took place in October, 2001. Working closely with the coalition members, RBH Media, a New York based media and design company, designed our website. Funded by the Open Society Institute and launched at *www.sitesofconscience.org*, this website links coalition member sites with human rights and social welfare organizations working on the contemporary form of the very issues raised at our sites. Visitors are invited to learn more about both the historic issues and the contemporary situation, and to participate in groups working to address the issues.

We also designed *Dialogues for Democracy*, the second phase of the coalition's work. Different at each site, these programs are designed to make more *explicit* what has always been *implicit* in our work – namely, that embedded in the stories we tell at our historic sites are lessons so powerful that, if taken to heart, they could improve our future. Each program engages visitors in a dialogue that makes explicit connections between the history of a site and related contemporary issues.

For example, most visitors to the Gulag Museum's restoration of the site of a former Stalinist labour camp and principal place of confinement for political prisoners from the 1930s through the 1980s, are Russians. Their country is in transition from a communist, totalitarian rule to a democracy. Although the bare bones of democracy are visible – there are courts, a parliamentary system, and free elections, for example – the historic mentality of enslavement and fear still informs the populace. The Gulag Museum is dismayed that there is no broad citizen involvement in the instruments of democracy and no tradition of voluntary, private watchdog groups. The museum wants to challenge this mentality and educate a new generation of Russians to cherish and participate in democracy by building civil society.

The questions the Gulag Museum's visitors will consider include:

- Why, between 1917 and 1991, did our society allow a majority of our citizenry to become victims of government abuse?
- Could Russia return to a repressive form of government?
- What institutions or activities are fundamental to a democracy? Which does Russia have, and what are the results? Which does it lack, and what are the consequences?
- How can I take responsibility as an individual for safeguarding democracy?

The Gulag Museum's *Dialogue for Democracy* program begins with an exhibit of Soviet propaganda materials, to demonstrate how the government brainwashed people. Then, through a film, the museum reveals what was really happening: the virtual enslavement of millions of citizens in the network of gulags to provide fuel for the industrialization of the Soviet Union and the repressive atmosphere that stifled free thought and action and incited deep fear and suspicion for generations. As most Russians do not yet understand it, the program will also clarify the difference between democracy and communism. The museum will also distribute *Power and People in Russia*, a cartoon pamphlet that offers a brief history of Russia from the tenth century onward. Using this history as a starting point, trained dialogue facilitators will engage visitors in the central questions throughout the program.

The Gulag Museum hopes to foster an engaged, educated citizenry. It seeks to fight historical amnesia, to be sure that voters do not allow power to be consolidated in a totalitarian regime again.

Each of the sites[1] has developed a similarly considered approach to the challenge of engaging its visitors in the contemporary implications of the historic issues raised at their sites. Each asks compelling questions:

- Has the welfare system gotten better or worse? (The Workhouse, England)
- What made it possible for racist violence and genocide to occur during the Holocaust, and is it possible that it could happen again today? (Terezin Memorial, Czech Republic)
- What can you do to help realize the country's funding goals? (Liberation War Museum, Bangladesh)
- How can I recognize injustice in what looks like a normal society? How can I act on it? (Memoria Abierta, Argentina)
- What forms of slavery exist today? (Slave House, Senegal)
- What will it look like when men and women are truly equal? (Women's Rights National Historical Park, U.S.A.)

HISTORIC SITES AS PLACES OF ENGAGEMENT

A new role for historic sites and museums is emerging. Every historic site representing the coalition is important, and their directors understand they are pioneering institutions. Every one of them embraces a mission that goes far beyond the simple chronicling of history. By coming together and further expanding our group, we hope to firmly and clearly articulate this larger mission, and thereby demonstrate the benefits of letting the mission be central to every aspect of a museum's behaviour.

In the coming year, the Tenement Museum plans to launch an Institute for Directors of Historic Sites to train coalition members in the use of history as a foundation for civic engagement. Members of the International Coalition of Historic Site Museums of Conscience are working toward the day when historic sites offer not only a deep sense of some aspect of history, but also assist the public in drawing connections between that history and its contemporary implications. We are conceiving of historic sites as places of engagement in which visitors, motivated to participate in finding solutions to enduring social, economic, and political issues, will be directed to organizations working in the field. We are mining and illuminating the power of history in an effort to improve the world.

ACKNOWLEDGMENTS

The idea of the Lower East Side Tenement Museum was conceived in my imagination. But many attended its birth and still more have nurtured it to this, its fifteenth year. Dr. Gerda Lerner, founder of the modern women's history movement, first opened my eyes to the power of history as an agent for social justice. My loving husband, Herbert Teitelbaum, supported me when very few saw any merit in the idea of a Tenement Museum. I am profoundly grateful to Anita Jacobson, who worked with me in the museum's early and somewhat desperate years, and to the distinguished group of men and women who lent their prestige to such a nascent and untried institution. These include William F. Kahl, the first chair of the board, as well as the first trustees Lisa Belzberg, Paul A. Crotty, Norman K. Keller, and Isabel C. Stewart. Renee Epps, senior vice president, has led the museum's day-to-day operation and the restoration for almost a dozen years with skill and humour. Senior Vice Presidents Liz Sevcenko and Katherine Snider have served as inspired leaders. Chief Curator Steve Long has lent his passion and determination to establish the nation's first collection of the material culture of the urban working-class and poor-immigrant experience. My associate Britta Graf's superb organizational skills make the organizational wheels turn smoothly and in a timely fashion. Preservation architects Roz Li and Judith Saltzman, of Li/Saltzman Architects, have lent their professional and personal talents to this path-breaking project. Pamela Keech's curation of the museum's historic apartments, and of the museum's annual benefits, has brought us renown. These are only some of the well over a hundred people now associated with the daily work of the Tenement Museum. Each and every one has contributed in a unique way to the museum's success. Then, too, the visitors, who come in increasing numbers year by year, have been truly instrumental in the creation of an institution that works for a broad cross section of people.

ENDNOTES

1 At its second meeting, the Coalition voted in the following new members: Angel Island Immigration Station; Auschwitz-Birkenau National Museum; Eleanor Roosevelt National Historical Site; Fort Sumner State Monument; Japanese American National Museum; Martin Luther King National Historic Site; Statue of Liberty National Monument/Ellis Island National Monument; National Civil Rights Museum; Thoreau Institute; Arbejdermuseet/The Workers' Museum; and the Women's Rights National Historical Park.

REFERENCE

Rosenzweig, Roy and Thelen, David
    1998   *The presence of the past: popular uses of history in American life.* New York: Columbia University Press.

OUR STORY IN OUR WORDS: DIVERSITY AND EQUALITY IN THE GLENBOW MUSEUM

Gerald T. Conaty and Beth Carter

A NEW APPROACH

On November 3, 2001, *Nitsitapiisinni: Our Way of Life* opened as a permanent exhibit at the Glenbow Museum in Calgary, Alberta, Canada. This 800 square metre (ca. 8,000 square foot) gallery presents the culture and history of the Blackfoot-speaking[1] people, as they know and understand it. It is the first significant modification to Glenbow's First Nations exhibits in over twenty-five years, and represents a change in both our curatorial knowledge and our approach to exhibit design. The project also represents an important evolutionary development in the museum's approach to community inclusion and participation in our exhibit and program-planning process. For the first time, a community was included as full partners in the development of an exhibit.

FIRST NATIONS AND MUSEUMS IN CANADA

By the late 1980s, many Canadian museums were inviting First Nations peoples to advise in the development of exhibits and programs. The Royal British Columbia Museum and the Museum of Anthropology at the University of British Columbia have had long-standing programs in which West Coast First Nations carvers were brought to these institutions to demonstrate their art and help interpret their culture (Ames

1992b, 1992d). The Head-Smashed-In Buffalo Jump archaeological site in southwestern Alberta was developed into an important Alberta Historic Site and tourist destination, and researchers consulted Peigan and Kainai elders about the past uses of the site (Brink 1992). In Regina, Saskatchewan, a Native Advisory Committee helped shape the development of the First Nations Gallery (Conaty 1989). The Canadian Museum of Civilization in Gatineau, Quebec has brought together First Nations people from across the country as they develop their First Peoples Hall. The Prince of Wales Northern Heritage Centre in Yellowknife, Northwest Territories (Janes 1982, 1987) and the Wanuskewin Heritage Park, near Saskatoon, Saskatchewan stand apart from these other examples; at these sites, the First Nations were included as major partners with museum personnel in the formulation of exhibit content and program development.

The late 1980s was also a time of a significant clash between First Nations and museums. The Glenbow presented *The Spirit Sings: Artistic Traditions of Canada's First Peoples* as part of the cultural events accompanying the 1988 Winter Olympics. It was targeted for a protest and boycott by the Lubicon Cree of northern Alberta, as these people were frustrated with a lack of progress in treaty negotiations with the federal government. Moreover, Shell Canada Ltd., the major corporate sponsor of the exhibit, was drilling for oil on land that the Lubicon claimed as part of their traditional territory. Linking these issues proved to be a successful strategy and captured the media's attention (Harrison, Trigger & Ames 1988; Harrison 1988; Ames 1992c). In a separate legal action, Mohawk individuals sought a court injunction for the removal of a False Face mask from *The Spirit Sings* exhibit. The court decided in favour of Glenbow, allowing the mask to remain part of the exhibit.

Museums suddenly found themselves to be the foci of political issues. In response, the Assembly of First Nations[2] and the Canadian Museums Association[3] struck the Task Force on First Peoples and Museums. After three years of deliberation, the Task Force, which included both museum professionals and representatives of First Nations communities from across Canada, presented a suite of guidelines that were intended to create institutions that are more inclusive and more welcoming (Hill & Nicks 1992; Nicks 1992). Among the key points was the recommendation that First Nations people be part of the planning process for the interpretation and exhibition of their heritage.

Despite the recommendations of the Task Force, it has been difficult for museums to move from consulting with First Nations to including them in full partnerships. In part, this is because our values and assumptions in the museum community give priority to scientific process and to the knowledge that follows from that process. We rely on historical documents and scholarly discourse for our information, and it is not easy to give equal value to traditional knowledge. (See Nadasdy 1999 for a discussion of the use of traditional knowledge in resource management.)

Just as modern museums reflect the structure and values of the societies that create them (Bennett 1996; Grasset 1996; Weschler 1995; Ames 1992a; Smith 1997), the relationship between Canadian museums and First Nations reflects the relationship within the larger society. Canadian writer and historian Michael Ignatieff provides an insightful discussion of this relationship:

> An imperial proclamation of 1763 recognized their (First Peoples') treaty rights, and hence their identity as separate nations, so bringing these people into a political confederation should have meant giving them equality as citizens while protecting their communal rights to be different. But that is not what happened…. Their pre-existing treaty relationships with settler peoples were ignored and their status as nations was dismissed.
>
> In retrospect, it is clear why this happened…. Rights were conceded when power was equal; rights were taken away when power flowed to the settler side…. When power relations changed, so did images of the aboriginal…. Racial ideology legitimized what sheer force had achieved. Expropriation and the denial of rights were then defended on the grounds that aboriginals were inferior….
>
> Thanks to the extraordinary historical tenacity with which aboriginal peoples have defended the memory of their nationhood and their treaty rights, the meaning they draw from the failure to assimilate them is clear: they must reacquire their rights of self-government and take responsibility at the individual and the collective level, for their destiny.
>
> This fundamental lesson, however, is still not accepted by the majority community in Canada. You could blame this on simple racism, but that would be to ignore the real problem. Assimilationist

policies would never have been pursued ... had settlers not believed that a political community must be composed of people who share the same values, culture, and assumptions, and that political equality can be accorded only to those who are recognizably the same. Shedding this belief is hard, for it is an ideal, not just a prejudice. (Ignatieff 2000: 58–62)

This presents two competing models of Canadian society. The one, held by the majority community, considers all citizens to be equal and that no group should hold special rights. The First Nations, on the other hand, posit that they have special aboriginal rights and privileges by virtue of their indigenous presence on the continent.

Public museums take their fiduciary responsibility to care for their collections on behalf of all of society very seriously. Special interest groups are rarely given privileged access to artifacts and the information about them. Similarly, we believe ourselves to be fora for open and equitable debate in which all sides of an issue are presented and explored (Cameron 1971) and we recoil when this debate is censored (e.g., Gibb 1997; Casey 2001). Whenever we do invite a *community* to join in the exhibit-development process, they are most often asked to participate as advisors, as their special knowledge contributes to the veracity of the content. Their individual stories add richness and meaning to the subject and bring connectedness to the visitor. But, in the end, the exhibit's content and the development process is defined by the museum as representative of society's majority community.

The First Nations' challenge to this model argues that the aboriginal rights, which put them in a special relationship with regard to such legal issues as land and resource use, also imply a unique position with museums as representatives of the larger society. They argue, as well, that their view of history has never been adequately presented to the public and that their understanding of their own cultures has been replaced by that of the anthropologist. In short, to equitably include First Nations within an exhibit requires a participatory model that goes beyond that of advisors or consultants.

We began the development of *Nitsitapiisinni: Our Way of Life* by explicitly recognizing these issues and focussing our discussions around them. Some of our museum colleagues, both within and outside Glenbow, suggested that to present only the First Nations' perspective is to abandon our ethical responsibility to present a balanced *truth* (see McGhee 1989 for an earlier discussion of this issue). However, we believed that the museum should take the opportunity to move away from a safe, neutral position if, by so doing, we could raise awareness and enhance the human rights debate. We knew from past experience the process by which communities could act as advisors; we did not know the process of involving people as full partners with the museum staff in the conceptualization and development of an exhibit. We did not know how, or even if, elements of Blackfoot culture could interact with elements of our museum culture to produce an intelligible result. Glenbow's senior management understood the social importance of the project and supported our experimental process.

The following discusses how we approached these issues as we sought a new way of working with a community.

Learning to Coexist

Quite soon after we began to meet, Rosie Day Rider (Kainai) shared her knowledge of Makoi-yohsokoyi – the Wolf Trail. It is summarized in the gallery:

> *Makoiyi*, the wolves, were the first *Ksahkomi-tapiksi* (Earth Beings) to help us. One winter, when our people were starving, a young man and his family camped by themselves as they searched for food. The wolves found the family and appeared to them as young men bringing fresh meat to their tipi. The wolves took this family with them, showing the man how to cooperate with other people when he hunted buffalo and other animals. The wolves told our ancestors that animals with hoofs and horns were all right to eat, but that animals with paws and claws should be left alone. The wolves disappeared in the spring, but we still see them in the sky as *makoi-yohsokoyi*, the Wolf Trail (the Milky Way). These stars constantly remind us of how we should live together.

Just as this ancient story taught Blackfoot people how to relate to one another and work together for survival, it stressed to us that the concepts of coexistence and respect must be key to both the content and the development of the *Nitsitapiisinni* gallery. From the beginning, all the participants were clear in their desire to see the development process as a true team partnership. At the very first meeting, community members stated that they were unwilling to participate if they were only to be considered advisors. Instead, they wanted to participate as full team members in all aspects of the story development, text and artifact selection, design, and installation of the exhibit.

For the purposes of this paper, the Blackfoot Gallery Team will sometimes be defined by the two components, the Community team and the Glenbow team. This division is useful to help distinguish the various roles of the team members, but in fact, we all worked together as partners. The community members were identified as content providers, building on traditional knowledge and rights to share that knowledge, and Glenbow staff agreed, as experts in exhibit development, to facilitate the translation of this knowledge into an exhibit. Together, the two groups formed a single Blackfoot Gallery Team with a common goal.

Interpersonal relationships are important in Blackfoot culture. Although they have adapted to working with Western bureaucracy, they prefer to develop personal relationships before initiating any business. This ancient tradition was reflected in pre-Contact and fur trading ceremonies in which gift-giving and feasting cemented personal relationships before barter and commerce proceeded. Glenbow began developing such a relationship in 1990 when we returned a Thunder Medicine Pipe bundle to members of the Kainai. Glenbow staff, in turn, were invited to ceremonies involving this sacred bundle. Ensuing years saw the connections with the Blackfoot deepen as more bundles were returned. This contact was primarily with Gerald Conaty, the senior curator of ethnology, who has also been asked to help facilitate the return of sacred bundles from other museums. With the formation of the *Nitsitapiisinni* Gallery Team, we recognized that it would be important for all members of the team to become personally acquainted with each other. Fundraisers, photographers, management, as well as curators, designers, and programmers attended our meetings with representatives from the four Blackfoot communities. Sometimes we had over twenty-five people at a meeting.

We often met in Fort Macleod, Alberta, a small town 150 km south of Calgary, where the Fort Museum kindly offered a basement meeting room as the venue for our meetings. Community members come from

Nitsitapiisinni: Our Way of Life has brought together museum staff and Blackfoot-speaking people together in a spirit of equality and mutual respect.

four reserves in southern Alberta and Montana, and Fort Macleod was central to their homes. Many people had to drive several hours to the day-long meetings, and it was often difficult to get everyone together in the same place. A cold basement in the Fort Museum would not seem to be the location most conducive to developing a vibrant and exciting story about the history and culture of the Nitsitapii, and their relationship to their territory. However, this was neutral territory for all of us. Glenbow staff were removed from our museum, from phones and other distractions. To reach the meeting, we drove through the plains of southern Alberta, often admiring the sun as it rose and warmed the beautiful countryside. Community members were still in the middle of Blackfoot territory but outside of their own reserves, where politics could be an issue.

Humour has a place in everything the Blackfoot people do, and our meetings were no exception. As we all became more comfortable with each other, there was much laughter and teasing mixed in with the serious discussions. Laughter takes away tensions, makes the work easier, and makes hard times more bearable. It also helps to cement friendships. Through much sharing and laughter, our team learned to work together, and in the process we have developed many lasting friendships.

Respecting Spirituality

Most of the Community team members are leaders in traditional sacred ceremonial activities. Their spirituality is intertwined with everything in their lives, including this exhibit project. Every team meeting started with a prayer to ask *Itsipaitapiyopa* (The Essence of All Life), the Above Beings, the Earth Beings, and the Water Beings to assist us with the meeting and, at the end of the day, another prayer was said to give thanks for the success of the meeting and to send everyone home safely. Glenbow team members were invited to many ceremonies during the exhibit development and attending these ceremonial occasions on the reserves was another way that team members could show support and learn to respect each other. The prayers, actions, songs, and protocols of ceremonies reinforced what the Community team members were sharing with us during our meetings. These ceremonies brought their ideas and stories alive.

Early in the process, Gerald Conaty and Frank Weasel Head (Kainai) suggested that the team sponsor a *Kano'tsissisin* (an All Night Smoke ceremony) to start our project off correctly. These ceremonies are held in the winter months, and pipe holders pray and sing sacred songs for guidance, success, and well-being. The ceremony starts at sundown and goes for most of the night, and includes a feast provided by the person sponsoring the Smoke. Arrangements were made to hold the ceremony in February 1999 in a hall on the Kainai reserve. Glenbow team members grouped together to cook roasts, ribs, potatoes, carrots, hard boiled eggs, and bannock, and to bring other food and drink. We asked Mae Tallow, a Kainai woman who is known for her spirituality and humility, to make the Saskatoon-berry soup, and Community team members provided the ceremonial tongue and ritual offerings. The president and CEO of the Glenbow Museum at the time, Robert R. Janes, sat as the sponsor, and two staff members, Gerry Conaty and Clifford Crane Bear, the Treaty 7 Community Liaison, acted as the ceremonial helpers, filling the pipes and serving tea and food. Cooking food and working for a holy event are acts of prayer.

Over twenty bundle keepers came to the ceremony to support our project, with about fifty spectators. To Glenbow staff, sponsoring a ceremony was a huge amount of work. But, as the wolves taught us, the team members worked together for the ceremony's success. It was also an amazing way to bring the essence of the Blackfoot Gallery to life.

Coming to Consensus

The goal for all decision-making was consensus. We quickly learned that we needed to run our team meetings in a very different manner. We could not pack the agenda. Sometimes we needed to spend the entire day on just one topic so it could be discussed thoroughly. We learned to listen to the silences. In the Blackfoot way, silence does not automatically mean *Yes*. It may mean, *I need to think about this for a while*. We learned to specifically ask each person for their opinion. It could take more than one round of asking, or one meeting, to reach consensus.

It took a long time to determine the title for the exhibit. Many titles were suggested over time and the team was keen to use their own language. However, the term *Blackfoot*, which is a direct translation of the word *Siksika*, was very controversial for some team members who felt it did not refer to the entire group. The term *Blackfoot Confederacy* has often been used, but the group wished instead to use their own name for themselves, which also has several variations. Much discussion ensued. We decided to focus on the term *Nitsitapii*, which means real people. However, the team did agree to the use of the term *Blackfoot* for marketing purposes, since they are commonly known by that name. Finally, the day came when we needed to make a decision for the full title. All possible titles were brought together, and team members brought some additional possibilities. As we went around the table, each person gave their ideas about the pros and cons of the suggested titles. Gradually some titles were rejected, and the entire team was comfortable with our final decision, *Nitsitapiisinni: Our Way of Life*.

In the traditional Blackfoot way, everything is taught through stories. Stories are for everyone, not only children. The lessons from stories can change as a person grows throughout life. Often, older people who are asked for advice will tell a story to put the issue in a bigger context. This gives direction without giving specific instructions.

For a long time, community team members presented their ideas for the exhibit by telling stories. It took many tries for the Glenbow team members to pull the key messages from these stories that could be used to build the gallery. (See Conaty 2003 for a discussion of this process.)

We learned to be patient as the Blackfoot-speaking team members had extensive discussions in their own language. This usually occurred when issues arose that concerned Blackfoot spirituality. Sometimes these matters involved information that is formally transferred through a ceremony and, therefore, could not be shared with the uninitiated museum people who were present at the meeting. In other instances, it was simply impossible to find English words for Blackfoot cultural concepts. English and Blackfoot linguistic structures are culturally based, and it is not always possible to find ways of expressing the abstract ideas of one culture in the language of the other. Once consensus had been achieved, museum team members were given a synopsis of the discussion and its conclusion. It is a measure of our mutual respect that these Blackfoot discussions were accepted by everyone as a matter of course. This process also shed light on the problems that must have arisen at the time of treaty negotiations between the Blackfoot and the governments of the United States and Canada.

BUILDING A CONTINUUM

Most Glenbow exhibits require about two years for completion. *Nitsitapi-isinni* took nearly four years. We are glad we built in lots of time, as we found that our concepts of goals, process, and content were continually challenged and reshaped by the Blackfoot members of the team.

We initially thought we would meet with a few Community members at a time. But the team requested that we all meet together, so all people could hear the different ideas and approaches. Some of the team members had participated in projects with other museums and not been satisfied with the end results. They felt that their information was modified or edited. They felt they had not been brought into the project early enough. Meeting as a large group, although not as efficient, meant that team members were always aware of the information that was being shared.

Most museums develop exhibits by setting goals, defining an audience, then developing a storyline. For this project, the two teams started with quite different goals. Glenbow wished to have a gallery that would attract visitors, primarily non-Native, and teach them about the history and traditions of Blackfoot people. We wished to display our rich collections and use the gallery for educational activities. On the other hand, the Blackfoot Community team wanted to share an authentic and accurate story of their history and heritage with their young people. They were very unhappy with how academics had treated them in the past, and took every opportunity to set us right. They saw this exhibit as a chance to correct misconceptions about their history for both Native and non-Native people. In the end, the two goals were combined and reworked into two new goals: to tell the Blackfoot story from their own point of view, and to focus the gallery on people who have little understanding of the Blackfoot, whether they are Native or non-Native.

As part of the goal setting process, Glenbow staff undertook front-end evaluations with museum visitors to the old First Nations galleries. We wanted to try to understand visitor expectations for the First Nations exhibits, and gain an understanding of visitors' existing knowledge. This evaluation was done through *knowledge mapping* (Derbyshire, Graham & Falk 2000; Falk & Dierking 2000). However, the process was not relevant to the Blackfoot community members. They were uncomfortable with tearing their culture apart for analysis, and instead preferred to think of every theme and idea as part of an interconnected whole.

Museum exhibits are designed to tell a linear story, which starts at one place and moves through time as the visitor walks through the gallery. Although everything is taught through stories in Blackfoot culture, these stories stress interrelationships of all things in Creation. Everything relates to everything else. Initially, Glenbow staff struggled to transform the stories and concepts being presented by the team into a linear storyline. The community members continually resisted this pressure, and through their great patience helped us to understand their approach. The exhibit became a series of non-linear themes and concepts, and repetition was accepted.

The gallery designers, Terry Gunvordahl and Irene Kerr, played a very important role in bringing the team's ideas to life. The final gallery design supports and furthers the themes and concepts by creating an environment which surrounds the visitor and which moves in a clockwise circle around the large, central tipi. Each theme area is connected to one another visually. Naturalistic flooring, warm colours, large photographs, large video screens and the use of wood, canvas, plants and animals bring the environment of the Blackfoot World into the museum in a tactile way. Artifacts are displayed in cases nestled into these environments. Stories are told in a circular, tipi-like room where the visitor can sit on curved benches or on a buffalo-fur robe on the floor. Trees, bushes, wall murals and soundscapes bring the family camp to life. Audio stations are scattered throughout the gallery, where Blackfoot team members tell anecdotes or stories in their own words and in their own language. The only area where you feel separated from the environment is in the historical period, starting with the formation of reserves. The isolation of the Blackfoot from their land into square houses and residential schools is dramatically reinforced by claustrophobic square rooms with low ceilings. In the final room, a circular space that is visually connected to the beginning of the gallery, the team looks to the future and stresses how the Blackfoot are taking control of their own destinies by combining traditional values and beliefs with contemporary life-skills.

LOOKING TO THE FUTURE

Nitsitapiisinni: Our Way of Life opened to the public on November 3, 2001, and the relationships we built with our team members continue. This is not the end of a project, but the beginning of a new phase in our relationships with the community, the team, and the public who will learn from our story.

Glenbow acknowledged several cultural, political, and historical issues of concern to the Blackfoot in developing *Nitsitapisinni: Our Way of Life*. Our harsher critics might see these as unreasonable concessions. First, we recognized that what has been written by historians and archaeologists largely represents a non-Native understanding of Blackfoot history. The Blackfoot have their own traditions about the past, which deserve to be heard. Second, anthropological discourse is not always an accurate portrayal of Blackfoot culture. Third, we accommodated the Blackfoot process of decision-making and adjusted our schedules as much as possible to allow enough time for adequate discussions of important issues. Fourth, we respected the Blackfoot protocol for establishing personal relationships alongside business partnerships. Fifth, we acknowledged the importance that spirituality plays in the culture and incorporated it into our gallery process.

These acknowledgments go beyond the level of any previous community involvement with the museum. We have shown this model to be workable and capable of producing a profoundly enriched view of the complexity of the historical and contemporary relationships between First Nations and the larger society. In the first year of the gallery, over six thousand students encountered the Blackfoot culture through our instructor-led programs. In responses to surveys, teachers have been overwhelmingly supportive. Visitors' comments, recorded in books at several locations in the museum, echo this positive experience. Over thirty-four hundred people from First Nations communities have visited the gallery.[4] Their comments indicate a strong pride in finding a museum exhibit expressed in a First Nations voice, and emphasize the importance of this exhibit in developing self-esteem for First Nations youth. We are all proud to have met one of the major goals of our community team members: to develop a place where First Nations youth can find cultural meaning and pride.

It is a joy to visit the gallery and see school children and visitors of all ages and cultural backgrounds interacting with the exhibit. We have had a wonderful response to the stories, and many people comment on how powerful they find the voices of the Blackfoot team members. The collaborative nature of the Blackfoot Gallery Team is very apparent to visitors. *Nitsitapiisinni: Our Way of Life* is an example of how traditional authority can and should have a place in contemporary Canadian museums.

It is clear that as cultural communities in our society learn to coexist, we all benefit as we begin to understand ourselves and our world in new and different ways. This can only benefit future generations in their struggle to find meaningful paradigms for their world.

Glenbow has redefined the fundamental nature of our working relationship with First Nations. This project, therefore, acknowledges the claim to special rights and a position of privilege voiced by First Nations.

If we accept the premise that museums reflect the larger society, then we can argue that Glenbow has addressed the issue of accommodating First Nations claims for special rights within the larger Canadian confederation.

ACKNOWLEDGMENTS

Many people contributed to the success of *Nitsipatisiinni: Our Way of Life*. The extended team members from Glenbow included Beth Carter, Gerald Conaty, Cliff Crane Bear, Irene Kerr, Anita Dammer, Terry Gunvordahl, Lynette Walton, Franklyn Heisler, Cindy Maurice, Gwyenth Claughton, and Ray Jense. Community members were Irvine Scalplock, Herman Yellow Old Woman, Donna Weasel Child, Clarence Wolf Leg, Frank Weasel Head, Andy Blackwater, Pete Standing Alone, Charlie Crow Chief, Rosie Day Rider, Louise Crop Eared Wolf, Allan Pard, Jerry Potts, Jim Swag, Jenny Bruised Head, Pat Provost, Earl Old Person, Tom Blackweasel, and Doreen Blackweasel. Robert R. Janes, who was president and CEO of Glenbow when the project was conceived, created a work environment that encouraged experimentation and innovation. His successor, Michael Robinson, found the funding that enabled us to realize our ideals. Mr. Tim Faithful, president and CEO of Shell Canada Ltd., saw the value of our project and provided substantial economic support. We thank Alberta Premier Ralph Klein for his support. Other funds came from the Department of Canadian Heritage, Alberta Lotteries, Alberta Community Enhancement Program, and Calgary Region Arts Foundation. Finally, we wish to acknowledge the ongoing support of Glenbow's Board of Governors.

ENDNOTES

1. *Blackfoot* is an Euro-American term which encompasses the Kainai (Blood), Siksika (Blackfoot), Amskaapipikanii (South Peigan or Blackfeet), and Apatohsipikanii (North Peigan) people who share a common language and other cultural practices. Each group has a unique identity, and there is no word in their language for the general term *Blackfoot*.
2. The Assembly of First Nations (AFN) is a political organization that represents the majority of Status Indians (that is, people whom the Government of Canada recognizes as of Indian descent) in Canada.

3 The Canadian Museums Association (CMA) is the professional organization which represents museums and museum workers in Canada.
4 A generous grant from Shell Canada Ltd. enabled First Nations people to visit the exhibit without paying museum admission fees for 2002 and 2003. This program has created greater awareness in the First Nations community within Calgary of the resources that Glenbow has to offer (Wright and Carter 2002).

REFERENCES

Ames, Michael
    1992a   De-schooling the museum: a proposal to increase public access to museums and their resources. In Michael Ames (Ed.), *Cannibal tours and glass boxes. The anthropology of museums*, (pp. 89–97). Vancouver: University of British Columbia Press.
    1992b   How anthropologists fabricate cultures. In Michael Ames (Ed.), *Cannibal tours and glass boxes. The anthropology of museums*, (pp. 89–97). Vancouver: University of British Columbia Press.
    1992c   Museums in the age of deconstruction. In Michael Ames (Ed.), *Cannibal tours and glass boxes. The anthropology of museums*, (pp. 150–68). Vancouver: University of British Columbia Press.
    1992d   The emerging Native view of history and culture. In Michael Ames (Ed.), *Cannibal tours and glass boxes. The anthropology of museums*, (pp. 77–88). Vancouver: University of British Columbia Press.

Bennett, Tony
    1996   The museum and citizen. In Tony Bennett, Robin Trotter and Donna McAlear (Eds.), *Museums and citizenship: a resource book. Memoirs of the Queensland Museum, 39*(1).

Brink, Jack
    1992   Blackfoot and buffalo jumps: Native People and the Head-Smashed-In project. In J Foster, D. Harrison, and I.S. MacLaren (Eds.), *Buffalo* (pp. 19–44). Alberta Nature and Culture Series. Edmonton: University of Alberta Press.

Cameron, Duncan
    1971   The museum, a temple or the forum. *Curator, 14*(1), 11–24.

Casey, Dawn
    2001   Museums as agents for social and political change. *Curator, 44*(3), 230–36.

Conaty, Gerald T.
    1989   Canada's First Nations and museums: a Saskatchewan experience. *The International Journal of Museum Management and Curatorship, 8*, 407–13.
    2003   Glenbow's Blackfoot gallery: working towards co-existence. In Laura Peers and Alison Brown (Eds.), *Museums and Source Communities. A Routledge Reader* (pp. 227–41). London: Routledge.

Derbyshire, P., Graham, K., and Falk, J.
    2000   Transforming the museum: New research on visitor learning and experience. Paper presented at the 95th Annual Meeting of the American Association of Museums. Baltimore.

Falk, John H.. and Dierking, Lynn D.
    2000   *Learning from museums: Visitor experiences and the making of meaning.* Altamira: American Association for State and Local History Book Series.

Gibb, James G.
    1997   The Enola Gay: learning from an unexhibited exhibit. *Museum News*, 30(2), 9.
Grasset, Constance D.
    1996   Museum fever in France. *Curator*, 39(3), 188–207.
Harrison, Julia D.
    1988   *The Spirit Sings* and the future of anthropology. *Anthropology Today*, 4(6), 6–9.
Harrison, Julia D., Trigger, Bruce, and Ames, Michael
    1988   Point/counterpoint: *The Spirit Sings* and the Lubicon boycott. *Muse*, 6(3), 12–25.
Hill, Tom and Nicks, Trudy
    1992   *Turning the page: Forging new relationships between museums and First Peoples.* Ottawa: Canadian Museums Association.
Ignatieff, Michael
    2000   *The rights revolution.* Toronto: House of Anansi Press.
Janes, Robert R.
    1982   Northern museum development: A view from the North. *Gazette (Journal of the Canadian Museums Association)*, 15(1), 14–23.
    1987   Museum ideology and practice in Canada's Third World. *Muse*, 4(4), 33–39.
McGhee, Robert
    1989   Who owns prehistory? The Bering Land Bridge dilemma. *Canadian Journal of Archaeology*, 13, 13–20.
Nadasdy, Paul
    1999   The politics of TEK: Power and the integration of knowledge. *Arctic Anthropology*, 36(1–2), 1–18.
Nicks, Trudy
    1992   Partnerships in developing cultural resources: Lessons from the Task Force on Museums and First Peoples. *Culture*, 12(1), 87–94.
Smith, Monica L.
    1997   Archaeology, museums and the creation of national identity in the India subcontinent. Paper presented at the Thirtieth Annual Chacmool Conference. University of Calgary, Calgary, Alberta, Canada. November, 1997.
Weschler, Lawrence
    1995   *Mr. Wilson's cabinet of wonder.* New York: Pantheon Books.
Wright, Beverly and Carter, Beth
    2002   Shell-sponsored First Nations admissions to the Blackfoot Gallery. First year summary report. Unpublished report, Glenbow Museum, Calgary.

ONE NATIONAL MUSEUM'S WORK TO DEVELOP A NEW MODEL OF NATIONAL SERVICE: A WORK IN PROGRESS

Joanne DiCosimo

In 1997, the Canadian Museum of Nature (CMN) began its current, concerted work to develop a new model of national service. Since then, we have followed a systematic process of consultation, analysis, pilot testing, and then further consultation and analysis. In April 2003, we began the formal implementation of the new vision, pursuing program and budget plans based on this new model. Of course, ongoing changes and refinements will be essential, but we have crossed a significant threshold. I will identify the premises or biases inherent in our decision to develop this new model of service, how we went about it, and our progress to date.

I should say at the outset that I believe that museums exist to fulfil social purposes and to meet social needs – that is why our museums were created, and it is why they are supported directly through government grants and indirectly through tax forgiveness.

I believe also that our primary challenge as people who work in museums is to establish the systems and outward-looking approaches to planning and budgeting that will ensure that our museums fulfil social purposes in an ongoing fashion. We need to establish methods and mechanisms not dependent on us as individuals, but systematized, because social needs change and evolve, and our museums need to change and evolve equally. Finally, I believe that being a national museum means creating the greatest possible benefit or value for the largest number of Canadians – that is at the heart of how we look at the social responsibility of this national museum. We are, and have been, engaged in a process of identifying the unique role of our museum and the areas where the particular bundle of assets we hold in trust can be of greatest service to Canada and to Canadians.

Many Canadian museum colleagues are familiar with the Museum of Nature's strategic planning process because they have contributed advice and ideas, and perhaps have assisted in one of the workshops or national consultation sessions. In this account, I will outline the process and results for each phase.

We began our first series of external consultations in the fall of 1997, travelling to six cities with as many CMN staff as the budget would allow. Our consultations were with colleagues in museums, universities, government and non-government organizations. We went with the following questions:

- Where can the national museum of the natural sciences make its greatest contribution?
- What is uniquely ours to do?
- Where can we be of greatest assistance in furthering CMN's and colleagues' mutual objectives?

From these sessions and from a series of internal consultations, we developed our strategic plan for 1998–2003, entitled *Focus and Renewal*.

The first objective in *Focus and Renewal* is "to increase national service and impact." Accordingly, in the period 1998–2001, we undertook a number of pilot projects to test potential aspects of a new national role. There were five primary pilot projects:

1. With the Bamfield Marine Station on Vancouver Island, we developed a joint staffing arrangement in an area of marine science of mutual interest, which allowed our research scientist to gain senior managerial and leadership skills. That two-year project concluded in the fall of 2001, and we then worked with Bamfield on the summative evaluation.
2. With the Royal Botanical Garden (RBG) in Burlington, Ontario, we undertook to develop jointly the national travelling

exhibition *Green Legacy*, which focuses on the endangered plants of Canada. The exhibition opened at CMN on May 9, 2002. Once the tour concludes and the RBG completes its major site redevelopment plan, the exhibition will become one of its permanent installations.

3. Working within the structure of the Canadian Museums Association, and with museum, zoo, and aquarium colleagues across the country, CMN convened the founding meeting of the Special Interest Group in Natural Science Research and Collections, which was held in May 1999 in conjunction with the CMA conference in Toronto. The group now has bylaws, a duly elected slate of officers, a system of ongoing communication thanks to the Canadian Heritage Information Network (CHIN), and administrative support from CMN.

4. Using CMN's location, our status, and our proximity to the federal government, we initiated work with the Natural Sciences and Engineering Research Council of Canada (NSERC) in two areas of critical importance to Canadian natural history museums: we chaired a committee of our colleagues, with · NSERC's support and assistance, to develop guidelines for the development, care, and disposition of the collections that result from NSERC-funded research projects; and we negotiated an agreement for financial support for a fellowship program to enable students of taxonomy and systematics to work at museum sites.

5. We completed the first draft of a Collections Development Plan. While the plan was developed for CMN, we kept in mind the broader context of the natural history collections held in various regions of the country. Again, the draft was prepared with the involvement and advice of colleagues across Canada, and as a discussion document it is now the focus of a next level of national consultation. The premise of this exercise is that the national natural history collection is the sum of all natural history collections held by Canadian institutions. The Canadian Museum of Nature holds one part and many others hold equally significant parts of the larger whole.

In June 2000, at the three-year point in the implementation of the current strategic plan, *Focus and Renewal,* we contracted two consultants to work with us to develop both a vision for the Canadian Museum of Nature in 2008 and the strategic planning process to achieve this vision in the five-year period 2003–2008. The goal was to envision CMN's service and value for current and future generations of Canadians; and I built in my bias of wanting to work to achieve this through the "family" network of the museums across Canada with natural history mandates.

There were two other fundamental givens in this process. The Canadian Museum of Nature is Canada's national museum of natural science. As a *national* museum we have a unique and special role. It is not enough to be simply a larger version of all of the other wonderful museums in Canada. There is a unique role and responsibility for the national museum: that is what we have sought to define and to realize. The other fundamental point is that CMN is a *museum*: that unique and special bundle, that intertwined ball of knowledge-creation, of collections development and the preservation of the physical record, and of public education and engagement. It is not a university, nor a department of government, although we clearly have overlapping interests in some areas, but a *museum*. As such, CMN is a part of a community of people and institutions across Canada that share our purposes, our interests, and our values.

I should like to outline briefly the process we undertook in developing a vision for CMN and to highlight some of our results. Clearly, in this planning process, we have built on all of the work, the thinking, and the learning that has been going on since 1997. The vision has been developing over time.

In June 2000, we held a workshop of thirty staff, our board, and eight invited guests (from universities, not-for-profits, other museums, etc.) to measure the public value of CMN's products and services. In this session we developed a working definition of public value, and we identified eight issues to be addressed in order to move forward. Six were internal issues, questions of "how" rather than "what." The other, fundamental questions were about the need to define CMN's national role and leadership role. That laid the ground for the focus on envisioning the unique role and service of the Canadian Museum of Nature.

From November 2000 to January 2001, Colin Eades, CMN's vice-president, and I interviewed forty colleagues across Canada in what

Creating a new vision of national service at a Canadian Museum of Nature staff workshop, June 2002.

our consultants called the *assessing readiness* phase. We found that there was real interest in working together to achieve larger purposes. Our colleagues had advice for us about both the substance of what we were trying to achieve and the approach that would make it successful: be sure your vision is bold, a stretch; focus in order to have impact; put it in an achievable time frame; the vision needs to be visceral – the head and the heart have to come together; emphasize mutual strengths and asset-building; have expectations of your partners. Only two colleagues declined to participate; one claimed not to be a team player, and the other said that Canada was not his museum's priority focus.

In addition to those external interviews, we also held two internal focus groups; there, too, colleagues confirmed a genuine interest in the opportunity to explore a new vision of national service. In February 2001, forty staff and six external advisors participated in the workshop *Laying the Foundation for the Vision*, the purpose of which was to define the elements of the vision of national role and service. From this workshop, we received messages of the importance of the museum being seen as a credible, trusted resource, accessible, and attuned to the public's interest in the environment and sustainability. In identifying the characteristics of the new vision, we used terms such as "enabling," "working together to create something that none of us can create on our own," and "creating the intersection between people and nature."

In April 2001, thirty-five colleagues responded to my invitation to work with us to develop the new vision of national service. A two-day *Building the Vision* workshop, part of the Canadian Museums Association conference in Ottawa, gave rise to four themes:

1. Partnership – proactively creating partnerships and networks across Canada.
2. Accessibility of resources, including knowledge, collections, expertise.
3. Canada's story – creating the larger context.
4. People – putting people into the equation, seeing people in relation to and as a part of the natural environment.

We did not have consensus on the international role or on a potential advocacy role for CMN, and these issues we took to the next session, an all-staff and board workshop held 18–19 June 2001. Staff exhibited a lot of energy and enthusiasm, but they also clearly wanted to know that they will be helped with training, coaching, and hardware, and not just expected to know suddenly how to work differently. There was much discussion of what it means to be a true partner and what it means to show or to be of concrete benefit to Canadians. There was a general consensus that international activity is appropriate where it is a logical outgrowth of national work. There was general agreement that we want to influence public policy, but do not want to mount public lobbies.

In addition to the cross-Canada consultations and workshops, two things informed the development of our new vision and strategy for national service for the future. The first was polling. Two different polls two years apart reinforced the fact that Canadians care deeply about the state and the future of our natural environment. In fact, polls indicate that the one thing we agree upon as Canadians is our pride in the physical beauty and diversity of our country, and we care deeply about the legacy we are leaving our children. Incidentally, the age group expressing the greatest concern for the future environment is that of the sixteen- to twenty-five-year-olds. What is striking is that that group is our lowest audience demographic. Here we have a group of people who clearly share the values of a natural history institution, and they are expressing these values in many ways (backpacking, hiking, working on reclamation projects), but they are certainly not expressing them by visiting natural history museums. Clearly, here is a direct challenge: How do we become meaningful to young Canadians?

The second and final thing that has informed the development of the museum's vision for the future is our interaction with potential contributors – donors, foundations, and interested corporations. We have known from the outset that creating the new future program and service will require resources beyond those available from government. In working to develop a fundraising capacity for the museum, two things have become very clear: first, funding and support are available if your services and your programs address issues that matter; and, second, funders want to work in partnership to create new products and services. Like museum colleagues and other government and non-government colleagues across Canada, funders want to work together to create things that none of us can achieve individually.

Finally, building on all of this valuable learning, the Canadian Museum of Nature has developed its vision for the museum in 2008. The overall theme is *Connecting People with Nature*, and we will work with partners across Canada over the next five years on projects that will engage and inform Canadians about environmental issues that are of interest and concern to us all.

The vision, which is available on the museum's website at *www.nature.ca*, has at least three primary component themes, which were first identified in the *Building the Vision* workshop in April 2001. Briefly, they are:

- Canada – to create the larger vantage or viewpoint;
- Partnership – to work with partners and through networks to create something together that none of us can create separately; and
- People – recognizing that we humans are a part of the natural world and key players in our natural heritage.

Goals and strategies have been developed to implement the vision. The five goals are:

1. To create and make accessible to the pubic relevant information about the environment and our place in it.
2. To contribute to building the capacity of Canadian natural history museums to respond efficiently and effectively to natural history issues of relevance to Canadians.
3. To provide vehicles to encourage public engagement in natural history issues and to contribute to informed public policy on those issues.
4. To develop CMN's internal capacity to work in integrated collaborative approaches.
5. To ensure that the project to renew CMN's main Ottawa exhibition site (the Victoria Museum Building) furthers the vision.

As the next step, a team of staff engaged in the nitty-gritty of how to put this on the ground. Development of the Implementation Plan has been focused in seven areas. First, there must be issues of relevance to Canadians. We contracted a national polling service to assist us in determining what natural science issues are of concern to Canadians (spring 2002). The results, combined with input from our scientific staff and the Strategic Program Advisory Committee, led to a decision to focus on environmental change. Second, we need forums. Having determined that we want to deal with issues of concern to Canadians, the logical program vehicle is one that provides the opportunity for obtaining information and exchanging ideas and perspectives. We have decided to learn to convene successful public forums, with a particular focus on engaging youth, the elusive group aged sixteen to twenty-five. In April 2003, we will launch our public education project on genomics ("The Geee! In Genome"), and we believe that the scientific issues related to this (stem cell research, cloning, DNA-based identity cards, genetically modified organisms) will provide ideal themes for our pilot-testing of the forum as a program vehicle. The next step in our learning will be forums delivered with partners at various locations in Canada using technologies to engage people across Canada. Third, we want to learn to be good partners. We want

The community monitors the river.

to learn also what ingredients make up the best partnerships and what are the necessary criteria for success. A task group of staff wrestled with these questions during a four-month period; with the assistance of our consultants, the group developed a partnership handbook to guide the institutional learning process. We debriefed our experiences with the pilot projects undertaken in 2000–2002, then selected two new demonstration partnership projects for the next phase of this work. One, the Saskatchewan Waterway Project, is the next evolution of CMN's successful community-based Rideau River Biodiversity Project. The other is a deliberate step into the less comfortable context of public–private partnership in a project to develop web-based educational and community-building resources. Fourth, we need to answer the question "how do we best use the constantly evolving technologies to achieve the vision?" We are grappling with questions of what is possible and where is the greatest potential for enhanced service and benefit to the broader scientific and public communities. The work to date has focused on commissioning a private-sector audit of current applications, contracting jointly with the

First governing board of the Alliance of Natural History Museums of Canada, January 2004. Left to right: Bruce Naylor (Royal Tyrrell Museum), Dave Baron (Royal Saskatchewan Museum), Don McAlpine (New Brunswick Museum), Pauline Rafferty (Royal British Columbia Museum), Johanne Landry (Insectarium de Montréal), Ed Krahn (Yukon Berengia Interpretive Centre), Joanne DiCosimo (Canadian Museum of Nature).

Canadian Heritage Information Network for a marketing study for a 3-D imaging lab housed at CMN, and creating a strategic technology plan to be fused with the five-year institutional plan for 2003–2008.

Fifth, the vision of CMN in 2008 is one of a national museum that works as a member of a network of museums across Canada to provide maximum benefit and service to Canadians. In this process, our objective is also to increase the capacity of all Canadian museums with mandates in natural history to provide social benefits. As a beginning step, representatives of eleven museums gathered on 4–5 October 2002 to explore the possibility of working jointly in areas where we would hope to make a difference or to have a greater impact through collective effort. In the workshop, we identified six potential areas: collections planning and development; creating the electronic specimen data record in formats that link with international biodiversity and research data networks;

creating the larger ecosystem or regional Canadian stories and creating richer products generally; increasing our ability to influence public policy and decision making; achieving efficiencies across our museum operations; and commanding increased funding for natural history museums. At this exploratory or founding meeting, three working groups were formed to develop a declaration of purposes for the national network and principles for its operation, to propose a governance structure, and to develop a draft project charter for joint projects undertaken amongst group members. The CMN will fund two years of operation for the network, in order to give members time to develop the method of working together, as well as to test and assess the value of this approach. And we have a name, courtesy of Bruce McGillivray, director of the Provincial Museum of Alberta: we are the Natural History League or the NHL. Sixth, formal plans were developed for both external and internal communications throughout the implementation of the five-year plan to achieve the new vision of service and benefit. I think that we all know from experience that there can never be too much emphasis placed on communication in any change process. Seventh, we need to determine what we are doing now that should continue, what should be modified, and what should be phased out. Further, we must determine what will be effective transition plans for these elements of our traditional program. Some work was done on this in the spring and summer of 2002. Most of the work was part of the process of planning in 2003, and is ongoing.

That is where we are in our effort to define a new model of service for this national museum. Some pieces are in place, because planning is like that: as soon as one begins to think in different ways, to envision the future concretely, then shifts begin.

The official start of our strategic plan for 2003–2008 was April 2003. Thus, all of the work to date has been preparatory. This extended period of preparation has been necessary and valuable. What we are striving for is a whole-system change. The sheer size and scale of this country, the numbers that are and should be involved, and the nature of the goal necessitate a methodical, deliberate, whole-systems approach. I believe that we have been thorough, sensitive, and also very persistent in our pursuit. As I have said repeatedly, this is challenging and it will take all of our very best efforts. If it were easy, it would have been done long before this.

It will take all of our best efforts to ensure that our focus is on the ends rather than on the means and to ensure that creating value for all Canadians remains the focus. I am very proud of what we have achieved together to date. I am proud of the staff of the Canadian Museum of Nature for their commitment, enthusiasm, courage, and concerted work to achieve the vision. And I am proud of our Canadian museum community for its vision and openness to working together across provincial and municipal boundaries to ensure that all of our museums are able to provide maximum value to Canadians. As I said at the outset, clearly this is a work in progress. Based on experience to date, I know that we will see it through together, that our Canadian museum institutions will be stronger, and that Canadians will benefit directly as a result.

ACKNOWLEDGMENTS

I want to acknowledge the staff of the Canadian Museum of Nature for their courage, commitment, professionalism and enthusiasm; Frank Ling and the Board of Trustees for their support, guidance and focus on serving Canadians in all regions; and my colleagues across the Canadian museum community for their participation, encouragement, expertise, and openness to working together to achieve the full service potential of these remarkable Canadian museum institutions.

ENGAGING YOUNG MINDS AND SPIRITS: THE GLENBOW MUSEUM SCHOOL

Michèle Gallant and Gillian Kydd

INTRODUCTION

The Glenbow Museum School is an educational program based on collaboration among the Glenbow Museum in Calgary, Alberta, local school districts, Chevron Calgary Resources (CCR, a wholly owned subsidiary of ChevronTexaco Corporation), the Calgary Foundation, and individuals in the community. In the spirit of collaborative enterprise, this article has been co-written by two of the participants. We will comment on four main areas of the program that we believe define its uniqueness: what makes this different from traditional field trips; the philosophy of the program and why we do it; the impact on the students, teachers, museum staff and parents; and the role in the community. Students, teachers, parents and staff who have participated in the program have also been given a voice through direct quotes, letters and journal entries.

PROGRAM DESCRIPTION

It is our belief that museums are public places with enormous potential for human growth and enjoyment. At the Glenbow Museum, the staff is encouraged to develop innovative public programs which are rooted in the community's needs and interests. Based on this approach, the

Glenbow Museum School is part of an educational partnership called the ChevronTexaco Open Minds School Program. The program is structured so that a class (grades one through twelve are eligible) spends an entire week at the Glenbow Museum, but unlike a typical museum field trip, the schoolteacher is the driving force behind the experience. To be accepted, the teacher must apply in the spring of the previous year with a written proposal explaining how Glenbow's resources will strengthen a long-term study project for their students. The intended study must last a minimum of a few weeks, but many last the entire year. There is no predetermined format for the teacher to follow, and virtually every part of the museum is accessible to teachers and students. Many Glenbow staff members contribute to the realization of the teacher's proposal, and these include educators, live interpreters, curators, designers, conservators, collection technicians, librarians and archivists. Community members, with expertise in writing, art, dance and music, are often invited to ensure that the experience is a meaningful one. The Calgary school districts provide two staff, the Education Directors, to administer the overall program and to give planning support to participating teachers.

Schools pay $600 per class for the week ($350 for high-needs schools) and this includes bus transportation from the originating school to the Glenbow, but the major portion of the costs, which average $3,500 per week, are covered by the program's business partner.

In addition to the Glenbow Museum School, the ChevronTexaco Open Minds School Program includes the Calgary Zoo School, the Calgary Science Centre School and the Cross Conservation Area. Campus Calgary, a sister program to Open Minds, has five sites, including the Inglewood Bird School, Canada Olympic Park School, University of Calgary School, City Hall School and Stampede Park School.

Glenbow's involvement in the ChevronTexaco Open Minds School Program began in the fall of 1995 with an eleven-week pilot project modelled after the successful Calgary Zoo School. Following the pilot, data gathered from two focus-group sessions, one with teachers and the other with parents, suggested significant impact on the participants. Teachers relayed how the program's constructivist approach deepened the learning that occurred at the museum and continued once the class had returned to school. The use of "real" objects, studied in exhibits that provided a context for them, increased the students' levels of discovery and the comprehension of connected and complex ideas. Parents who accompanied their child's class to the Museum School described how their relationship with their child had grown because of the program. Through the sharing of rewarding and personal experiences, parent and child had connected on a higher level. Even dinner conversations changed as the children enthusiastically recounted their adventures.

Based on the strength of the data, the Museum School became an institutional priority and funds were designated to operate the program for a year until a business partner was secured. Through the generosity of Donald Harvie and the Devonian Foundation, a space in the heart of the museum's fourth floor exhibit area was renovated and architecturally transformed into a stimulating classroom befitting its purpose. Unlike many of the classrooms found in museums, this one is not relegated to a basement or down a long hallway, but resides equally with the exhibits. The real classroom, of course, is the museum itself.

Every spring, twenty-eight teachers' proposals are accepted to the program, and planning for implementation begins in early July with a three-day workshop, and continues until each class moves to the museum to begin their week. The goal of the week is to provide unique, interdisciplinary studies which allow students to explore the museum and to experience what they discover through their senses. We believe enhanced learning occurs when students are exposed to, and immersed in, exciting and personalized experiences that reinforce their school studies. Workshops, reflective time, sharing, and writing and sketching in personal journals assist the student in understanding his or her world. Remarkable changes in the attitudes and behaviours of students and in their beliefs about museums, themselves and the world around them have been noted after they have participated in this process. Many teachers say that the program has been the highlight of their teaching careers, and that it is has been instrumental in the development and rejuvenation of their teaching practice.

WHAT MAKES THIS DIFFERENT FROM REGULAR FIELD TRIPS?

Glenbow Museum School is a very different approach to teaching that uses the museum as a catalyst for extended, deep learning. The main differences from a regular field trip are ownership and the extended period of time at the museum. The visit itself is an entire week, and the students are immersed in this rich and new world. The extended time gives the students a chance to calm down and to get over that initial period of excitement and apprehension that happens in a new environment, so they can really learn.

Ownership

Unlike conventional field trips, there is true ownership by the teacher and the students. Traditionally, school programs are based on a museum educator's interpretation of the school curriculum and sometimes, but not always, on consultation with teachers or curriculum specialists from schools. Rarely is a program co-developed, assessed, and continuously refined, or even rewritten by museum educators and teachers working together in a symbiotic relationship. In lacking meaningful collaboration, the programs may be based on the museum educator's beliefs and perceptions of what teachers want and need. This speculation may be reciprocated, with teachers thinking they understand all that the museum has to offer. Relationship building between museums and teachers allows the status quo to be exceeded, resulting in unique, meaningful and memorable experiences being integrated into the lives of the thousands of young people who participate.

Most school programs give the museum educator control over what happens in the museum, but this does not ensure that the teacher's expectations of the program will be met. As one would expect, we have observed that teachers are very adept at assessing the needs of their students, and only when armed with this information can the museum educator provide what is required from the museum's resources.

Frequently in museums we see teachers playing a passive role, often more concerned about student behaviour than being fully engaged in the educational experience taking place. In contrast to this, the Museum School model invites teachers to create the learning experience from its inception. The teacher initiates the project by writing a proposal for a long-term study and submitting it to the museum for consideration and, in all cases, begins the study at school. It intensifies during the week at the museum, and finally it is brought to completion back at the students' school of origin. Areas of study can be conceptual, such as the exploration of Time, or curriculum-based, such as a study of Calgary's history. No two weeks are completely alike, because the teacher has created their students' week according to their perception of their students' learning requirements. The subject or theme chosen, and the approach to understanding it, belong to the teacher. Museum staff play a supportive role in the realization of this concept, as do the parents and other individuals who accompany the classes. The work continues at schools for many months, as what the students experienced weaves in and out of their studies. There may be a culminating activity, such as creating a class museum with personal objects, or perhaps it is a way of demonstrating their learning about curriculum topics, such as Ancient Greece or the regions of Canada.

The surrendering of their safe and secure traditional roles does not always come easily, for either teachers or museum educators, especially with the challenge of engaging students for an entire week in an unfamiliar and intimidating environment. This is where trust and the process of true collaboration between professionals from different disciplines come into prominence.

Time

The other major difference from traditional field trips is the extended time at the museum and the time given the students to make sense of the rich environment in a personal way. The week at the museum gives the students a chance to calm down and get over the "novelty effect" that Falk & Dierking (1992) describe so they can really learn. It is human nature to be nervous and excited when one arrives in an unfamiliar place. Thus, on Monday of the week at the Glenbow, the students spend time getting to know their surroundings. This means that they are more relaxed on the following days and can focus on learning, and by Friday they "own" the museum. We know how important it is to give the students long periods of time each afternoon when they can visit exhibits and study artifacts of their choice. The number of programs or presentations is kept to one per day. We work hard to help the classroom teacher understand that "less is more." The teacher has been helped to teach the skills of looking deeply at art and objects, and of drawing, well before the class arrives for their week at the Glenbow. It is a common sight throughout the museum to see students deeply engrossed in writing and drawing in their hardcover journals. The gift of time, the sense of ownership and the integration of the week into the school year, make Glenbow Museum School a very different experience than a regular field trip.

WHY ARE WE DOING THIS?

The School View

It is so important for school-based educators to realize that Museum School is not a frill or an add-on. In fact, the learning that occurs is fundamental to what schools hope to accomplish, not only the specific knowledge, skills and attitudes that appear in most curriculum documents, but also the larger goals that should be met through education, such as critical-thinking skills, curiosity, and creativity.

Even the most talented teacher can only accomplish so much within the four walls of the classroom. We know that children need to be engaged in interesting, meaningful ideas and experiences in order to learn. It is the thinking of Howard Gardner (1991) and Eleanor Duckworth (1987) which supports the basic idea of our program, which is that children are capable of deep, powerful learning if you can provide them with a stimulating and rich environment, skills with which to communicate, and choice. In short, children learn best when there is a reason to learn. For example, just as babies learn to speak because they have a need to communicate, students learn to write better when they have important things to say.

Another crucial element of learning is choice. We don't all see the world through the same lens, so providing students with the opportunity to choose what to focus on, gives them ownership. For example, we encourage teachers to leave enough flexibility in their daily plans so that their students can spend one or two hours each day in the exhibit areas of their choice, studying objects or art. Since museums house thousands of works of art and artifacts, they are perfectly suited for free-choice learning. Some students may be drawn to the Asian Art, while others may spend long periods of time in *Nitsitapiisinni: Our Way of Life*, the Blackfoot Gallery. A senior high school class of thirty ESL (English as a Second Language) students, whose homelands included Somalia, Sudan, Iran, Vietnam, Cambodia, Afghanistan and Lebanon, astounded us with how quickly they personalized the museum. Sometimes they found artifacts from their country of origin, while other times they found artifacts similar to ones they had known or used. Their discoveries generated excitement and dialogue among their classmates and heightened self-awareness, self-esteem, and self-confidence, as if their past life in their previous country and their present one in Canada converged in this experience. The respected Glenbow Museum had acknowledged and therefore validated their previous lives, and those of their families.

These marvellous environments in the museum also have interesting people working in them who can build upon what the students are experiencing. The classroom teacher is the most important person in the learning equation, but the staff at the museum can work collaboratively with that teacher to make the experience even better. In this way, students get to meet people such as curators, archivists, designers, and writers. These are people who are passionate and knowledgeable about what they do, and they open up new worlds for our students.

The Museum View

The power of the museum environment cannot be overestimated, because amidst objects from countries and cultures, past and present, lies the potential for deep learning that informs the mind and the body for a lifetime. Contemplating a work of art or an historical artifact sparks curiosity, questions and awe. Personal interaction with "a thing" combines the logic and rigour of science with the creative powers of the imagination, and can also activate the intuitive self. During the course of a week at the museum, school children, teachers, and parents can be observed in deep states of profound reverie. Realizations emerge, are noted in journals and later enthusiastically shared with others in the class. This type of reflective practice is stimulating to the mind and spirit, and it challenges and expands personal boundaries in a safe way. Even previously silent children are motivated to share. One grade three teacher described her class's highest learners as jumping higher, and the strugglers as working harder, because they were all motivated after being to Museum School. The building of self-esteem is an important by-product of learning in a stimulating and nurturing environment, and one that is adaptable to a variety of learning styles.

During the pilot stage of the Museum School program, we were concerned that the quiet surroundings of the museum would not stimulate

Students discussing a work of art in the Glenbow Museum's art gallery.

the grade eight students who would be attending. Some of those students were from a low socio-economic part of Calgary, and had never been to a museum. They were also street-wise and a few were known to carry weapons. The teachers at the school assured us that no weapons would enter the museum, and to our knowledge, none did. This was because the students *wanted* to be at the museum and understood that getting caught with a weapon would mean staying at school. What was surprising in the follow-up assessment was that the students said they liked the tranquility of the museum most of all. They felt that in the museum they could get away from the crowds and the noise, which was so much part of their everyday school experience. They could be by themselves; they could be themselves.

WHAT IS THE IMPACT?

Through ongoing assessment of the program and the collection of anecdotal data, there is considerable evidence to support the notion that this program has a substantial impact on students, teachers, parents, and other family members, as well as on Glenbow staff.

Impact on Students

The extended work at the students' regular school, followed by a week at Museum School, stimulates students to develop their abilities to observe in multi-sensory ways, and to think critically. Teachers tell us they are impressed by the depth of learning that takes place at the museum, and how it impacts learning once the students are back at school. Subsequent field trips to the museum and other sites have more meaning because students know how to observe more fully and are motivated to engage in the experience. Through specially designed programs, reflective time, and sharing, students discover a better sense of how they belong in the world and how their values and ideas can be part of an interconnected worldview. As the week progresses, there is a heightened sense of confidence as the museum becomes a personal place where students develop a sense of ownership and stewardship of their own experiences in the museum. Perhaps this is why teachers describe how their students are able to move in the community in a way they have never done before, especially in a place like a museum, where they would have normally felt excluded.

That "ownership" of Glenbow brings with it an awareness of the workings of the museum. Depending on what the week has held, students may know what a curator does, how chemistry plays a role in restoration, what the archives consist of, or the how exhibits are designed. The *learning to see* results in students having new lenses with which to view the world. They have learned to slow down and to make personal connections to new experiences. They have also learned how to communicate their ideas more descriptively through writing, drawing, and perhaps through movement or sound.

Cathy Cochrane's research (2000) demonstrated a significant improvement in writing skills with young students with our program. She tested twelve classes of grade three students, half of whom participated in the Open Minds program. She had them do a writing task in the fall, and then a second writing task four months later, when six of the classes had participated in the program. An outside marker, using the Alberta

Achievement Test rubric, assessed the writing. The writing achievement of the control group increased by an average of six percent, but in the classes that had taken part in the Open Minds program, the writing skills rose by twenty-four percent, a fourfold increase. Of course this wasn't entirely due to being at a site for one week, but due to the cumulative effect of having the classroom teacher working on open-ended descriptive writing connected to interesting experiences.

The Impact on Teachers

Teachers say the program allows them the opportunity to explore new educational approaches, as well to observe and learn about their students in ways they cannot do in the regular school classroom. Many teachers tell us coming to Museum School has been the highlight of their teaching careers, and that it has revitalized their passion toward education and their profession. Some recount how the program has forever changed their teaching practice. When you think about it, this is the ultimate form of professional development. The teachers are encouraged and supported to work in new ways with their students and the community, but the process is "hands on." This isn't a series of workshops, but actual practice with their own students. There is a high level of support from the time they are selected to participate, from the summer workshop, to planning assistance from the school district's education directors for what they do at school, to working closely with Gallant to plan the week's schedule. During the week itself, they have support from Gallant and the other staff at Glenbow. They are not left to fend for themselves.

The teachers who participate are at many stages on the continuum of teaching practice, but the advantage of the program is that teachers can enter at their own level. Their thinking may be shifted in small, basic ways. For instance, some may still be seating children in rows in their classrooms, but the Museum School classroom is organized so that the students are seated in groups at tables. These teachers thus begin to see the power of student talk and collaboration. Another example is that all teachers are encouraged to have small, hard-covered journals for their students, so they can begin to work in them many weeks before they come to the Glenbow, and then use them for the most important part of each day at the museum, which is the writing and drawing about the objects and the art. The teachers learn that their students produce far better writing from open-ended journal writing than from filling in worksheets. They also learn that students get more from constructing their own meaning from their experiences than from having a program "delivered" to them.

For other teachers, the shifts in their thinking can be fundamental to their entire philosophy of teaching. For instance, they begin to see curriculum not as a list of objectives, but as major, overarching ideas with many entry points. They begin to understand that their students are creative, thoughtful people who see the world in unique ways. Time and again we hear teachers say that they cannot believe that certain students are thinking and writing in such depth. Often the students who have difficulty learning in a traditional setting are the ones who shine at the Museum School. Behaviour is seldom an issue, because each child can find his or her own path of learning.

Something else that happens to teachers is personal learning. The three-day summer workshop immerses them in the world of the museum. They become learners themselves as they have sessions on writing, drawing, and critical-looking techniques. When teachers are curious and creative people, that passion is reflected in their students. We hope that these new learnings for teachers will translate to their regular classroom teaching, but it is not easy to evaluate the impact on teachers. Questionnaires and focus groups have given us some information, but fundamental changes are harder to detect. Kydd's doctoral research followed one teacher over several years, and more closely during the year in which she participated in the Glenbow Museum School. She discovered that this teacher gained a great deal of confidence, and her beliefs about teaching and learning became more solid. She has become a leader, modelling this approach for others within her school and within her school district. Museum School does not appeal to all teachers, but those who choose to participate discover that they are energized and excited about their career.

Impact on Parents

Parents and other family members also play an important role in the Museum School. Some parents have taken an entire week off work in order to share this experience with their child, and grandparents have even come from out of town to be with their grandchildren, making this program an intergenerational one. In a focus group session, several parents related how their relationship with their child had grown through this deeply meaningful experience. Conversations between adult, child, and often siblings have been initiated, providing an opportunity to both learn from and about one another.

One of our favourite stories is about a father who was a trucker and had never been inside the Glenbow. He told us how he had helped to move the collections to the present building years earlier, but had never realized how interesting it was inside. When his son participated in Museum School, he came every day to volunteer, bringing an extra lunch for a child in his group who often went hungry, and even driving another child downtown when he missed the bus. At the end of the week he wrote a lengthy entry in the classroom teacher's journal, thanking her for her hard work and the experience she had provided for his son. He pointed out to us the students lying on the floor in an exhibit, writing in their journals. "Look at that! This should be part of public education – the government should pay for this!"

Impact on Museum Staff

Each year, twenty or more Glenbow staff, including collections technicians, curators, conservators, archivists, librarians, First Nations Liaisons,[1] writers, educators, visitor services personnel, and live interpreters, contribute their time and expertise to the Museum School. Students and teachers are awed by the depth of their subject knowledge and by their obvious enthusiasm and passion. In turn, the staff feel valued and are energized by the students' curiosity and desire to learn more about the staff's particular subject area. Staff responses show the depth of their commitment to this program and to the museum's mandate for excellence in education.

THE ROLE IN THE COMMUNITY

Glenbow Museum School is unique in that it has developed a level of trust among the many partners. The primary collaboration is between the school districts and the museum, but other partners from the community are integral to the success of the Museum School. As described earlier, our major business partner is Chevron Canada Resources, which covers a large portion of the costs. The late Donald Harvie, past chairman of the Devonian Foundation, and a driving force behind the program, figured largely in the initial funding. At first, we were somewhat nervous about having a business partner, but Chevron Canada Resources is a strong supporter of what we are trying to accomplish in education. They truly are a partner, not just a sponsor, and they trust us to accomplish the education goals of the program. The company has given the program a much-needed profile within the community, and the partnership strengthens our voices within the school districts.

Not long ago at the Museum School, a grade five student read a story to his class that he had just written. The three main characters of the story were inspired by sculptures in the museum. Each of the characters was mighty and powerful, but not strong enough to do a certain job. Only by working together were the characters able to gain the necessary force to reach their goal. Perhaps there is a parallel here between the story and the Museum School. Its three main characters are the Glenbow, teachers, and a business partner. While each contributes individually to the community in positive ways, it is only by joining forces that they are able to rise above their individual strengths to even greater accomplishments. Effective collaborative ventures require a great deal of energy and patience, but the tremendous rewards are well worth the effort.

As mentioned earlier, there are currently nine sites using this model in Calgary. With the support of Kydd and the program's education directors, the number of sites grows steadily both in Calgary and beyond. In Edmonton, there are four sites using this model; they include the School at the Legislature, Petro-Canada Zoo School, Provincial Museum School, and Edmonton Oilers I.C.E. School.

Across Canada, there are schools at the Vancouver Aquarium, Moncton City Hall, and at the Canadian Medical Hall of Fame in London, while in Lansing, Michigan, there are schools at the Michigan Historical Museum, Michigan State University, and the Potter Zoo. The International School in Singapore also uses this model at four community sites, including the Singapore Zoological Gardens, the Jurong Bird Park, the Museums of Singapore, and the Singapore Science Centre.

As the Glenbow Museum School continues to thrive, and the umbrella program continues to expand, this concept of schooling within the community is beginning to serve as an exciting model of what education can be. The old model of isolated classrooms and teachers needs to change. The old model of the isolated museum needs to change. We have shown how these two worlds can work together with powerful results.

ENDNOTES

1 Glenbow Museum established the First Nations Liaison position in 1994 to facilitate communication between the Museum and First Nations communities. The liaison contributes traditional knowledge to the cataloguing, care and maintenance, and interpretation of the ethnological artifacts. This person also plays an active role in developing and delivering programs and exhibitions. Firsthand knowledge of issues that are key to the Native community and personal experience results in the development of more dynamic and relevant programs.

REFERENCES

Cochrane, Cathy J.
    2000   Creating thoughtful writers. Unpublished Master of Education thesis, University of Portland, Portland, Oregon.
Duckworth, Eleanor
    1987   *The having of wonderful ideas and other essays on teaching and learning.* New York: Teachers College Press.
Falk, John H., and Dierking, Lynn D.
    1992   *The museum experience.* Washington, D.C.: The Compass Press.
Gardner, Howard
    1991   *The unschooled mind.* New York: Basic Books.

LIBERTY SCIENCE CENTER IN THE UNITED STATES: A MISSION FOCUSED ON EXTERNAL RELEVANCE

Emlyn H. Koster and Stephen H. Baumann

INTRODUCTION

A productive new consciousness seems to have at last gained a foothold in the museum field – one that, simply put, calls upon museums to be focussed as much on their usefulness as on their popularity. But this is not a new calling. In his concept of the "new museum" that accompanied the founding of The Newark Museum in New Jersey in 1909, John Cotton Dana (1856–1929) advocated: "learn what aid the community needs and fit the museum to those needs" (Dana 1999). Museums might arguably have taken this step sooner, and with less anguish, had Dana's writings been more available in the years after his death (Weil 1999).

The American Association of Museums (AAM) was founded in 1906. Three-quarters of a century would pass before the profound intent of Dana's philosophy began to resurface (American Association of Museums 1984, 1992), leading to a national initiative in 1998 to examine and encourage the civic engagement of museums (American Association of Museums 2002). A scholarly assessment of trends in the U.S. museum field over the late twentieth century has concluded: "The field shifted from internally focused and collection-driven organizations to externally focused and market driven organizations with greatly broadened stakeholders" (Harvard University, John F. Kennedy School of Government 2001).

The Canadian Museums Association (CMA) was founded in 1947. In 1995, its joint conference in Montreal with the Société des musées québécois had the theme *Museums: Where Knowledge is Shared*. Its publication recalled the 1972 and 1989 declarations of the International Council of Museums (ICOM) in Chile and The Netherlands that museums are a powerful force for human development and places where the public can look for the meaning of the world around them. However, in the same paper (Koster 1995), it was concluded that the missions and perceptions of most museums are, in fact, rarely reflective of such declarations. In 1996, at the symposium marking the 150th anniversary of the Smithsonian Institution, Harold Skramstad challenged museums to adopt mission statements that go beyond what the museum collects, preserves and interprets to explicitly state what the museum's beneficial outcomes are intended to be in community terms (Smithsonian Institution 1997). The president of the Canadian Museums Association has recently wondered: "Are we really interacting with our society or are we just pretending to do so in order to soothe our conscience?" (Brousseau 2003).

This book focuses on the museum field with respect to the trend of social responsibility. The term is now entrenched as a summary descriptor of concerted efforts by for-profit and non-profit organizations to improve society and undo harm where harm has been done. Taking a broader perspective, we need to remind ourselves that efforts to improve the human condition must be combined with efforts to improve the condition of Planet Earth in environmental terms (Leahy 2003) for its urban, rural and wilderness areas. In the new calling, therefore, it is incumbent upon all types of museums – natural history, human history, art, science, and technology – to become reflective about their external relevance to pressing human and environmental contexts.

The dictionary defines relevance as relating to the matter(s) at hand. Synonyms are meaningful, pertinent and symbiotic: antonyms are self-absorbed, detached and elitist. In the museum context, being truly relevant demands identification of external challenges to which the museum's expertise can be directed and make a positive difference. It is not simply a matter of trying to engage the community in what the museum wants to do (Carbonne 2003). Rather, it needs to be about a wholehearted externalization of purpose.

The following recent developments beyond the non-profit field help us to understand the profound implications of the relevance concept. In corporations, there is a spectrum of consciousness from self-interest to the common good (Barrett 1998). Barrett points out that movement across this spectrum is preferably driven by the organization's internal desire to be beneficial to the world as well as to be profitable, but organizations are commonly obliged to adopt this philosophy because of financial difficulty or external pressure. Leaders of organizations are being called upon to be social activists, establishing and clarifying the social agenda for their organizations (Parston 1997). The alignment of these lines to philosophy and practice in the museum field is explored elsewhere (Koster 1999). Richard Barker (Barker 2002) has delved into the point of leadership and, referring back to Aristotle's philosophy, develops the fundamental premise that it is, at the core, about harmonious pursuit of positive consequences in the world. This is similar to the Japanese ethical principle of "kyosei" which encourages individuals and organizations to live and work together for the common good (Barrett 1998). And further in this regard, Stephen Covey (Covey 1990) usefully distinguishes the meaning of efficiency and effectiveness; he considers efficiency to be about doing things right and effectiveness to be about doing the right thing. In a graphic metaphor, Covey talks about efficiency in terms of how well you climb a ladder, whereas effectiveness is about in which direction you first decide to lean the ladder. In the increasingly popular field of performance metrics (U.S. National Center for Nonprofit Boards 2001b), it is much easier to quantify efficiency than effectiveness. For museums, while it may be tempting to compare visitors per square foot per year among museums as an efficiency indicator, if the visitor's learning experience is peripheral to the challenges and opportunities facing that community, then this metric says nothing about the museum's effectiveness. *In Search of Excellence* was a best-selling business book first published in 1982 (Peters & Waterman 1982). In hindsight, it was focused on efficiency aimed at maximum corporate profits. Today's definition of organizational excellence revolves around the common good, about doing the right thing, about effectiveness.

Certainly, museum expertise is well suited to help educate the public on the daunting array of challenges facing the world today (Worldwatch Institute 2003). These include: inter-cultural friction; the need to lift the horizons of disadvantaged communities in meaningful and sustainable ways; environmental stewardship and slowing the decline in biodiversity, as well as the depletion of natural resources; coping with constant societal evolution because of technological advance; thinking long term and in the big picture about our past and present actions; and educational reform that harnesses the value of all community resources. Increasingly, museum professionals are airing their thoughts about the greater usefulness of their institutions in society (e.g., Koster 1995, Casey 2001, Weil 2002, Brousseau 2003, Worts in press).

As importantly, museums should also be places where humanity's positive activities inspire us. These include: reduction in the rate of our population growth; enhanced disease prevention and other medical advances; the development of technologies that help to overcome disabilities; the greater availability of communication technologies; the progress toward universal gender equality and civil rights; the commitment to foreign aid; the rise of environmentalism and increased research into renewable energy sources; increased availability of learning resources; and the value we place in conserving historically valuable structures. With the word "museum" having its roots in Greek "as the place of the Muses," we should remind ourselves that the institution of the museum is a unique and enduring one that is fundamentally for reflection and insight.

Science-technology centres have in many ways accelerated the relevancy movement in museums (Koster 1999). The reasons include increased flexibility in the absence of a defining collection, the need to devise exhibitions and programs explicitly for a public education purpose, the application of new technologies that extend the reach of the museum, the fact that their core subject matter is a primary driver in the progression of society, and an increasing reflection on the optimal niche of this type of museum in the infrastructure of how people acquire their knowledge about science and technology.

Introduction to Liberty Science Center

North America's first major science museums were the Franklin Institute in Philadelphia and Museum of Science and Industry in Chicago, opening in 1824 and 1933, respectively. The Museum of Science in Boston and the California Museum of Science and Industry in Los Angeles, now the California Science Center, both opened in 1951. The first institutions devoted

The Liberty Science Center is located along the Hudson River, next to the Statue of Liberty.

exclusively to interactive learning experiences were the Exploratorium in San Francisco and the Ontario Science Centre in Toronto, both opening in 1969. Reflecting a rapid increase in popularity of this new kind of museum, the Association of Science-Technology Centers, based in Washington, D.C., was founded in 1973. The Canadian Association of Science Centres (CASC) is a strengthening, newer entity for national advocacy and collaboration. Today, virtually every American state and Canadian province is well served by ASTC or CASC member institutions.

New Jersey's Liberty Science Center is situated in a state park on the Hudson River shore in Jersey City, opposite lower Manhattan, and next to Ellis Island and the Statue of Liberty. This 170,000 sq. ft., non-profit institution was conceived in 1980 as a helping hand to the region's education and workforce development. It opened in January 1993, following a US$68 million collaborative, private- and public-sector campaign.

Lying between New York City and Philadelphia and rising westwards towards the Appalachians, New Jersey is America's most densely populated state and culturally one of its most diverse states. Although New Jersey has the highest percentage of postgraduate degrees in science and technology, the nation's top high-school graduation rate, and highest average household income, almost one in ten of its citizens live below the poverty line. Liberty Science Center is New Jersey's most popular museum, and the only New Jersey destination listed in New York City tourist guides and authorized for field-trip use by New York public schools. Our host community of Jersey City is a fast-growing part of the New York metropolitan region, and is well served by light-rail, ferry, and subway mass transit systems. Its Hudson shorefront is a glistening, new, high-rise cluster of businesses and residences with new hotels. Behind this skyline are revitalized residential streetscapes, but inland many of its low-rise neighbourhoods are in an economically depressed, and still only slowly improving, condition.

Mindful of this regional socio-demographic picture, Liberty Science Center's mission is to be *an innovative learning resource for lifelong exploration of nature, humanity and technology, supporting the growth of our diverse region and promoting informed stewardship of the world.* Multimedia learning environments consist of themed floors on the environment, health, and invention, the largest IMAX® dome theatre in the United States, and one of its few 3D laser theatres.

Although its early years were financially unstable, the Center's proactive role in the community and region became a solid foundation for strong recovery and enduring growth, thereby enabling its tenth anniversary in January 2003 to be a time for much celebration. Today, it is known for an unusually varied suite of onsite, offsite and online educational programs that are intertwined with exhibitions and aligned with state and national curriculum standards at each grade, its great diversity of audience, the frequency of its voice in both conferences and in the literature on the trend of science centres to be more useful institutions (e.g., Schiele & Koster 2000), and its community services in the aftermath of the terrorist attacks on the World Trade Center (Koster 2002).

This article profiles three of Liberty Science Center's mission-driven learning experiences, each unique in the museum field, and each with a strong flavour of social responsibility. Each follows the same format, first framing the matter at hand, then describing the program in response to it. All three also incorporate educational technologies to a degree not typical in the museum field. At Liberty Science Center, we strive to use the resources and collaborations that result from value-added application of networked communication technologies that invigorate the learning of science. We subscribe to the view that technologies connecting home, school, the workplace, and institutions of learning offer unparalleled opportunities to provide access to science education, strengthen learning and teaching, and sustain lifetime learning, no matter where and no matter when.

Following these illustrative program profiles, the article concludes by reflecting on the recent trend of social entrepreneurship in non-profit organizations, and on how a museum's sustainability is strengthened by active adoption of a socially responsible mission.

EXAMPLES OF A SOCIALLY RESPONSIBLE MISSION IN ACTION

Reaching Underserved Audiences: Abbott Partnership Program

Science centres, many of which are located in urban settings and dedicate themselves to science learning opportunities for all, face no greater challenge than the attraction, involvement, and retention of underserved audiences (Falk 1998). In its early period, Liberty Science struggled to find ways to serve the school and family audiences from its most challenged communities, including its host community of Jersey City. With a public school enrollment of thirty-two thousand, fewer than a thousand were using Liberty Science Center each school year. The surrounding districts of Newark, Hoboken, and Elizabeth, each less than ten miles away, were equally detached from the learning opportunities that we offered.

Liberty Science Center started to develop its Abbott Partnership Program in 1997 for the state's most educationally at-risk districts. A New Jersey Supreme Court ruling in the Abbott vs. Burke case addressed inequities in educational funding by establishing a new and permanent extra funding stream intended to improve academic performance in these schools.

We were challenged to find a partner with significant financial resources and unquestioned commitment to science learning for underserved audiences. The obvious collaborator was the New Jersey Department of Education. It manages the educational reform efforts in place in the thirty Abbott districts. We convinced both education officials and policy advisors to the state governor that our programming would add value to their science improvement initiatives. We were not in search of a handout, but instead stressed our desire to earn their financial support through collaborative involvement with science education reform. We demonstrated how our field trip, travelling science and videoconferencing curriculum materials were all aligned with, and supportive of, New Jersey's core curriculum content standards. We demonstrated how our teacher professional development workshops, institutes and professional days were attuned to the emerging state certification requirements. We suggested the inclusion of a third emphasis on the family, to extend school and science centre learning into the home. We offered to provide families with a free family pass for use at Liberty Science Center, a quarterly newsletter, and monthly community evenings as part of an inclusive package of science education services. The state legislature welcomed this comprehensive program as a novel approach that matched the strengths of the science centre with the needs of their constituents.

This education initiative has been recognized for its innovation in the museum field, winning the social responsibility award for the year 2000 from the New York Society of Association Executives. Through a yearly grant-in-aid from the state government, Liberty Science Center has been enabled to provide students, teachers and families from these districts with a menu of onsite, offsite and online experiences that address the science education needs of these underserved communities. During the 2001–02 school year, 159,711 Abbott district students (91,316 through onsite programming, 62,800 through offsite, school-based programming, and 5,595 through online videoconferencing) benefited from our programs. Also, 1,063 Abbott district teachers participated in school day, weekend, and summer professional development workshops. Over twenty-five thousand family members from Abbott communities used their free family pass to enjoy the excitement of a Liberty Science Center visit. Annual program funding has increased from US$1.7 million in 1997–98 for the three largest districts under direct state government control, to US$6.0 million for the total of twenty-eight Abbott districts in 1998–2000, to US$6.6 million since the start of the 2000–01 school year, when twenty-eight grew to thirty eligible districts. Even in the toughest of times for the economy of New Jersey in 2003, support for the Liberty Science Center's Abbot Partnership Program was sustained at US$6.1 million. This also comes at a time when it seems almost universal, at least across the United States, that governments are cutting back on their funding of cultural institutions quite significantly.

Key to the management and delivery of these programs is the articulation of a yearly service agreement between Liberty Science Center and each district. Ahead of each school year, our staff travel to each district where they meet with district leaders, curriculum specialists, and principals to construct a menu of interactions that use science centre resources to support school and district science learning objectives. This mutually generated contract identifies which students, teachers, schools, grade levels, or classrooms will benefit from the state-sponsored interactions. In these discussions, we fashion many distinctive strategies focused on grade levels across a district, individual schools, teams of teachers, exceptional students, or special projects. Key to these conversations and the agreements that result is the recognition that customization of our science learning offerings is an innovation that brings the greatest value to our school partners.

Teachers from Abbott district schools are now active participants in our ongoing professional development activities. Implementation of the Abbott teacher ambassador program is a chief reason for the increase in their participation. There are 423 schools in the thirty Abbott districts. In each school, we have identified an ambassador who acts as our liaison for all student and teacher interactions. Armed with an electronic mailing list, website resources, and an ambassador tool kit containing detailed support materials and scheduled events at Liberty Science Center, these ambassadors are establishing strong, year-round bonds for us in each Abbott school. Their presence and the ongoing interactions that take place directly between us and schools are responsible for an important shift in perception which has moved our offerings from traditional supplementary resources to an integral resource that contributes to the school science program.

Liberty Science Center's commitment to the provision of outstanding science education experiences for New Jersey's Abbott district students, teachers, and families has helped redefine our educational and institutional programs. We are energized by the learning opportunities that arise when we collaborate directly with teachers, principals, and district leaders. We are elated to see the joy and enthusiasm when Abbott families from many different cultures experience their first onsite visit. We are ecstatic to see students engaged in a curriculum-aligned discovery challenge, an electronic field trip, or a cow's eye dissection, and know that we are making a positive impact on science learning. While the Abbott Partnership Program has enabled us to bring much value to the science education needs of our community, we are most proud of the changes we have undergone as a result of the value the community has brought to us.

Prior to the establishment of the Abbott Partnership Program, Liberty Science Center was essentially serving only the more affluent parts of the surrounding region. Now, our reach is broad and our ability to make a difference in the science learning of all of our constituents is greatly enhanced.

Also critical to our success was the identification of a new place for Liberty Science Center in the too-often distinct worlds of informal and formal science education. Tradition identifies the science centre as the domain of informal learning, while schools occupy the domain of formal learning. The New Jersey Department of Education oversees the world of formal K–12 education, and to become a serious partner with them we had to demonstrate that we understood, and could operate within, this domain. Demonstrations of our expertise in inquiry-based learning and science content were not enough to win them over. Presentation of Liberty Science Center as a dynamic learning environment was impressive, but did not speak to our ability to work in schools with students, teachers, and principals to support their science-learning objectives. We had to demonstrate our expertise on issues related to core-curriculum

We have reshaped all that we have to offer and have convinced decision-makers in formal education of our ability to add value within their system.

standards, learning frameworks, school-reform models, teacher professional-development requirements, and student achievement. We had to rethink and articulate the role for a science centre in the world of formal science education. We were successful in reshaping all that we had to offer so that the decision-makers in formal education were confident in our ability to add value within their system. Many science centres are also capable of finding this place for themselves.

Like most science centres, Liberty Science Center is perceived as an interactive and engaging learning destination for schools and families. To succeed with the state-wide Abbott Partnership Program, we had to enhance this perception so that our audience saw us as an interactive and engaging learning resource. Significant aspects of our work with the Abbott districts could not take place onsite. Bus transportation is problematic, and teachers will only travel so far and so often for professional-development opportunities. To make an impact across all thirty Abbott school districts, it was necessary to fully engage in technology and travel to make our educational resources totally accessible. This commitment to a portfolio of onsite, offsite and online science-learning experiences sets the stage for students, teachers and families to interact with the science centre every day, instead of once or twice a year. This new self-image prepares science centres to compete and thrive in a new, wired and more competitive science-learning infrastructure.

Tackling Youth Smoking: The Unfiltered Truth

The statistics are stark, yet stupefying. With so much science generating so much data, how is it possible that the use of tobacco continues to be the number-one adolescent public health problem in the United States? Well over a quarter of all high school students in grades 9 to 12 are smokers, along with almost 15 per cent of all eighth graders (U.S. Center for Disease Control 2001). Each day, more than five thousand additional young people try smoking for the first time, and another more than two thousand become daily smokers (U.S. Department of Health and Human Services 2001).

In 2000, the tobacco companies spent US$59.6 million in advertising expenditures for the most popular youth brands in youth-oriented magazines. Spending from the recent master settlement between the federal government and major tobacco companies has not reduced youth exposure to advertisements for these brands. Magazine advertisements for the brands reached more than 80 per cent of young people in the United States an average of seventeen times each during the year 2000 (King and Siegel 2001).

Spurred by the urgency to decrease the diseases and deaths that result from smoking, and supported by funds made available through the above-mentioned national master settlement agreement, the New Jersey Department of Health and Senior Services sought innovators to join their comprehensive tobacco-control program. Liberty Science Center jumped at the opportunity to become a partner in the effort to reach fourth to twelfth graders with a message about the realities of youth smoking.

An initial visit to see firsthand Liberty Science Center's diverse youth audience and innovative educational programs in May 2000 convinced the Commissioner of Health and Senior Services that we were right for the task at hand. The Commissioner saw the science centre teeming with eager learners, while live videoconferencing connections brought science educators on the exhibit floors to remote New Jersey classrooms. We also explained that travelling science educators were in schools doing assembly programs, classroom workshops, and dance performances to illustrate the science of muscles and bones. With a yearly youth audience exceeding 450,000, one-third of which represents the most underserved communities in New Jersey, Liberty Science Center was viewed as a unique resource whose contribution to the battle against tobacco would complement already established community partnerships, cessation programs and media campaigns.

During the summer of 2000, program developers and science educators began to pinpoint the concepts and goals that would form the foundation for our program. Research, focus groups, and brainstorming scrutinized existing tobacco-education programs and helped to identify a distinct niche for us that would build on our strengths and not replicate existing endeavours. Four key goals became the basis for the development of the content and delivery of our program: 1) decrease the acceptability and initiation of tobacco use among those aged 9–17; 2) increase youths' understanding of the harmful effects of tobacco use and the creation of tobacco products; 3) increase awareness of the negative effects of smoking in community and personal settings; and 4) increase the awareness and knowledge of how the tobacco industry uses strategic marketing to mask the negative aspects of tobacco use and tobacco products.

During this development process, it seemed to us that one initiative or experience would not suffice. We wanted to create a set of integrated experiences, each able to stand on its own, so that our youth audience was presented with multiple opportunities, in a variety of media, to interact with our anti-tobacco messages.

In October 2000, we submitted a request for funding to the Department of Health and Senior Services for our tobacco-education program entitled *The Unfiltered Truth*. A US$783,000 grant was approved for development and implementation, with funding beginning on January 1, 2001. Our program has three components and all were actively underway during the 2001–02 school year.

Extreme Choices is an onsite, 3D laser show written by playwright Michael Hollinger and co-produced by Lightspeed Design Group and Liberty

Science Center. Fifteen minutes long, the show presents an adolescent in an arcade playing a new, high-tech game called *Extreme Choices*. Urged on by his peers and intrigued by the promise of a prize when he successfully finishes the challenge, the young player and the audience face a dwindling set of choices as the game progresses. The game takes command, much like a burgeoning nicotine addiction, until fantasy becomes a bit too close to reality and all involved are uncomfortably engulfed in the strong anti-smoking message. While *Extreme Choices* is the name of the game, it is about simple choices of when and how much to smoke that lead to extreme consequences down the road. Crafted to send home only one or two important ideas, the show uses the power of the visual and aural environment to first engage the audience in the game before switching to become a tool to drive home the show's climax. Over two hundred thousand youth guests have seen *Extreme Choices*.

Hot Air is a forty-five-minute dramatic production, also written by Michael Hollinger, that is performed in middle schools throughout New Jersey. Co-produced by Playwright's Theater of New Jersey and Liberty Science Center, the play features six professional actors who portray three middle-school students and six adults in a story that meshes smoking, athletics, advertising, and family relationships. Jessica is a budding track star who cannot seem to quit smoking. Her father is in advertising and has a new cigarette company account that wants to promote smoking among teens. Numerous conflicts start to emerge, and with humour layered throughout the story, the audience is entertained and informed about the evils of both smoking and the corporate deceit behind tobacco sales and marketing. In this play, the audience sees character development and understands more intricate storylines; things that are not possible in an experience like *Extreme Choices*. In *Hot Air*, the dramatic medium allows multiple messages about issues related to smoking to be explored and resolved. After each show, the cast takes questions from the audience, and whether performed in a gym, cafeteria or auditorium, it is clear that the key messages in the show are coming across loud and clear. *Hot Air* was performed over 190 times during the 2001–02 school year, and will be seen at 235 shows during the 2002–03 school year. Over eighty thousand students will see *Hot Air* during its two-year run.

The Science Behind Tobacco is an extensive website (Liberty Science Center 2001) providing information, images, links, and interactives about the cultivation of tobacco, the manufacturing of cigarettes, and the health effects of tobacco use. Intended for both youth and adult viewers, the website provides classroom guides for both *Extreme Choices* and *Hot Air*, while presenting science background information that elucidates the relationship between the tobacco plant, the cigarette maker, and the nicotine addiction that leads to serious health consequences. Unlike the more temporal and location-specific constraints inherent in a play and a 3D laser show, *The Science Behind Tobacco* website is a readily available resource able to be explored and visited at the user's discretion. The website first appeared in November 2001 and in the first year, there have been 180,000 unique visits.

A critical component of *The Unfiltered Truth*, the entire program, was an extensive evaluation effort conducted by The Conservation Company from Philadelphia, Pennsylvania. We worked with them to develop a variety of survey instruments that enabled us to collect both quantitative and qualitative data from surveys, interviews, and focus groups to measure the impact of this tobacco education program. The evaluation effort collected data at the science centre, in schools, and through an online instrument on the website. Data collection and analysis were completed in June 2002. The evaluation indicated that each component was successful in delivering a strong anti-tobacco message. Students understood that *Hot Air* and *Extreme Choices* were about choices, and that the choices characters made were similar to the choices children believe they have to make in their lives. Students reported that both the play and the 3D laser show demonstrated how poor choices lead to bad health consequences. Most importantly, the data indicated that the greatest impact of *Hot Air* and *Extreme Choices* was to help students understand the negative impacts of smoking on health and well-being. *The Science Behind Tobacco* was rated highly as an interesting, easy-to-understand, well-produced website for research and learning about tobacco and the health effects of smoking (The Conservation Company 2002).

Liberty Science Center's tobacco-education program received high marks from the Department of Health and Senior Services and our viewing audience. Additional funding was received to extend the run of *Hot Air* through the 2002–03 school year, and to develop three new multimedia interactives for *The Science Behind Tobacco* website. Many schools that booked *Hot Air* during its initial run have rebooked for the 2002–03 school year, and have also visited and seen *Extreme Choices*. Indications are that the website is serving as a valuable adjunct in support of the two other initiatives, and providing important content for both student and teacher learning. The presentation of a comprehensive program about tobacco use through initiatives that hit hard and true has offered a unique opportunity for conversations that are relevant and socially responsible. For us, commitment to telling the straight story in innovative and thought-provoking ways about the nation's number-one public health issue is the essence of our mission.

Learning from a Hospital Operating Room: Live from … Cardiac Classroom

Liberty Science Center provides experiences that seek to make a difference in young lives by making science and technology understandable. Whether crawling in the pitch-black tunnel to come to terms with sensory deprivation, holding a hissing cockroach to get close to nature, constructing something from parts in our invention area, or exercising in our bodies-in-motion area, our young guests are immersed in audio, visual and kinaesthetic experiences that are unique and memorable.

For all science centres, and for museums generally, building on such successes with young learners to make an impact on high-school students is an ongoing challenge. Mere multi-sensory interactions with the rudiments and objects of science and technology are not the experiences most likely to inspire the next generation of science thinkers and doers. For older students, it is critical that the presentation of science is seen as a human endeavour of mind, spirit, and activity that is integrally linked to addressing individual and societal challenges. Creating ways to incorporate real things, real processes and real demonstrations of science that present the most current science thinking, research and practice provides the most certainty that high school students will become engaged with the world of science and technology.

Liberty Science Center's *Live from … Cardiac Classroom* is an innovation that succeeds in meeting this challenge. Through the weekly presentation of live, open-heart coronary-bypass surgery, students from rural, suburban and urban schools come onsite to interact with science and technology as it happens. The patient, the surgical team, and the students are immersed in a real life-and-death drama. Whether because of genetics or a combination of lifestyle choices, the patient's future is intertwined with multiple aspects of science and technology. For most, the excitement and relevance of science learning has never been so real. Whether contemplating the patient and issues related to illness and recovery, or the surgical team and issues of knowledge, skill, and preparation, students are moved by the experience. Inclusive of the learning strengths we attribute to exhibition, mediated programming, and the appropriate use of technology, *Live from ... Cardiac Classroom* provides high school students with an extraordinary and compelling experience that they will never forget.

Live from ... Cardiac Classroom is a program that uses two-way videoconferencing technology to connect seventy-five middle or high school students at the science center to a cardiac surgical suite at Morristown Memorial Hospital, twenty-five miles away in mid-northern New Jersey. For two hours while open heart coronary bypass surgery is in progress, students are immersed in a unique learning experience that extends their knowledge and understanding of anatomy and physiology, lifestyle choices that determine health consequences, the diversity of careers in the medical field, and how research and new technology are changing the health and medical professions. Well prepared through access to web-based, standards-aligned curriculum materials, students interact directly with all members of the surgical team to better understand the teamwork, experience and differentiated skills required to mend a malfunctioning heart. Our educators, audiovisual staff, and volunteers facilitate the audio and video interactions while surgical instruments, materials, and devices circulate around the room and questions come in a steady stream from the engaged audience.

Begun in 1998 as a result of the imagination of Liberty Science Center trustee and practising cardiologist William A. Tansey III, MD, *Live from ... Cardiac Classroom* is a regular feature of our weekly school-year programming. As of January 2003, we have presented 210 surgeries, usually five or six per month, reaching eleven thousand students and other guests. An annual allocation of US$50,000 for technology upgrades, materials, and supplies, plus in-kind investment on the part of the hospital, now support an initial equipment and set-up investment of US$350,000. Two-thirds of our student participants pay US$15 to attend, and one-third participate free of charge as part of our service to underserved school districts.

Live from ... Cardiac Classroom uses two-way videoconferencing technology to connect middle and high school students to a cardiac surgical suite.

It often begins in the same way. *Live from ... Cardiac Classroom* uses two-way videoconferencing technology to connect middle and high school students to a cardiac surgical suite. The multiple plasma screens and the audio feed go live and the students are greeted with an operating room scene not unlike *ER* or from the Learning Channel on cable television. Blue-green gowns, high-intensity lights and a flurry of activity may make one think that you are watching television or a pre-recorded video. Then, in a split second, it changes. "Good morning, Liberty Science Center. Today, we have a 47-year-old female, overweight, a lifetime smoker, with no history of heart disease in her family. We anticipate doing four grafts today, but we won't know for sure until we see the heart.... I can see we have a full room today: tell me a little about your class and your school."

Even with a visit to the website and classroom lessons in preparation for the surgery, students now understand that they are participating in something remarkable and unique. This is not a simulation or an edited for television medical procedure. *Live from ... Cardiac Classroom* is the real thing, and for the next two hours the sights, sounds, knowledge, interactions, and feelings that accompany authentic experiential learning will be elevated as each student becomes a participant in the drama. Our work to engage guests in impactful, experiential learning uses many modalities. Exhibition offers information, objects, and interactives in support of free-choice exploration and discovery. Mediated programming adds the human element, to facilitate and guide learning and investigation. Technology breaks through the boundaries of time and space to enhance the breadth and depth of what we offer. *Live from ... Cardiac Classroom* creatively combines the strengths of each of these modalities to present a learning opportunity like few others.

A unique collaboration is required to present and sustain *Live from ... Cardiac Classroom*. Three partners – Atlantic Health System, Mid-Atlantic Surgical Associates, and Johnson & Johnson – work with us to maintain the educational excellence and programmatic distinctiveness of what we offer. Atlantic Health System is our hospital partner that supports the technology infrastructure in the operating room, the dedicated T1 videoconferencing connection to the science centre, and all the members of the medical team except the surgeons. Mid-Atlantic Surgical Associates is the surgical practice whose four doctors donate their time and expertise to make their surgical suite and our videoconferencing theatre a dynamic learning environment. Johnson & Johnson is our corporate sponsor, whose annual funding and counsel enables the sustenance and growth of the innovation. The American Heart Association is a new contributor of program enhancements.

Partnerships are key to the success and excellence of so much that we strive to accomplish as institutions of learning. For five years now, science educators, doctor/scientists, hospital administrators, and corporate professionals have pooled their resources and found the common ground and mutual commitment to learning. The whole is now literally much greater than the sum of the parts. Partnerships of this degree and longevity are rare, but when they do occur, significant endeavours result from the collaboration.

Science centres, museums, and all institutions of learning are facing change and stress as they try to come to grips with the proper role for emerging, networked communications technologies as a learning tool for the future. Over the past decade, as we have experimented with websites, webcasts, satellite links, remote cameras, and videoconferencing, we have struggled to find meaningful and cost-effective applications. Prototypes and temporarily funded experiments have come and gone, with few meeting the tests of fiscal and programmatic sustainability. *Live from ... Cardiac Classroom* has not only survived, but continues to prosper and evolve as it matures. Why this application of videoconferencing succeeds while so many others fail is simple and significant. *Live from ... Cardiac Classroom* is fundamentally about an extraordinary learning experience: it is not about the capabilities and coolness of videoconferencing technology. Its instruments, environment, content, messages, and people are the primary and special elements of the learning experience. The technology that enables the opportunity is less important. All along, the contributions from each partner in the collaboration have focused on the learning goals as paramount, and the intricacies of the technology as secondary.

Liberty Science Center strives to be an innovative resource for the lifelong exploration of nature, humanity and technology. *Live from ... Cardiac Classroom* is a signature embodiment of the integrated learning experiences that we develop to ensure that we achieve our mission. Engagement with this program provides a window into our commitment to relevance, social responsibility, and the growth of our diverse region. Establishing connections for learners that make an impact and promote further thought and investigation is the benchmark for relevance. This program connects with students, and provides images and ideas that connect what they have been told with how they live their lives. They see for themselves how choices to smoke, eat poorly, or ignore physical fitness will lead to potential health consequences. Vivid images and answers to their own questions help make this link. *Live from ... Cardiac Classroom* provides the opportunity to make these messages real for a teenage audience that is seldom moved or affected by words, books, or the advice of teachers or parents.

New Jersey is often referred to as the "medicine cabinet to the world." Many major pharmaceutical and medical technology companies are headquartered in our state. Liberty Science Center was formed through efforts of corporations and research institutions to help stimulate the growth of science and technology professions that are so critical to the economy of New Jersey. *Live from ... Cardiac Classroom* provides a consummate and unmatched opportunity for career education. From the first moment to the closing suture, students see a real view of the world of work and the teamwork that is required to achieve excellence. Each professional on the surgical team takes a turn with the microphone to share with students the education, professional training, and responsibilities required by each job. These conversations have stimulated students to now see the roles of surgeon, physician assistant, perfusionist, medical technician, researcher, instrument designer, and science educator as equally interesting and viable career options.

Learning that inspires young adults to examine their lifestyle choices and think ahead to entertain professions in science and technology exemplifies how this program advances our institutional mission. Too often innovations like *Live from ... Cardiac Classroom* find their implementation and impact with those who have the resources to invest. Many underserved students and schools miss the opportunity to be part of these initiatives. We are proud that this program provides us with another opportunity to promote the growth of our region for all of its citizens, not just those who have the resources.

In 2002, *Live from ... Cardiac Classroom* garnered the prestigious single annual Award for Innovation from the worldwide Association of Science-Technology Centers (ASTC), a program co-sponsored by U.S.-based BBH Exhibits/Clear Channel Entertainment. In addition, an adjacent mini-theatre presentation of the operating room experience in its four main aspects – i.e., surgical procedure, tools and equipment, anatomy, and career paths – for all other visitors has garnered five awards, including one from the American Association of Museums.

REFLECTIONS FOR THE MUSEUM FIELD

Although one may be convinced that the search for relevance is a prudent one (Covey 1990, Koster 1999), the question arises: Does the pursuit of relevance also lead to growth in a museum's operating resources?

We submit that the foregoing program examples of Liberty Science Center solidly indicate that this is indeed the case. That is, if a museum positions itself so as to attract sustainable external resources on the basis of its declared and clear added value to the outside world, then the museum clearly develops a more secure financial footing. The opposite is clearly also true – who wishes to fund irrelevant activities? It is, however, the case that there continue to exist museums, and to a lesser extent science centres, where earned and contributed funds support missions that are oriented more to internal interests than the common good. If a museum is generously supported by endowment revenue and/or by grants from philanthropists whose interest lies in a more classical museum mission, then it is entirely possible for that museum to continue to live in an internally focused mode, oblivious to any external accountabilities.

Other types of informal learning institutions have shown the trend towards heightened external consciousness more graphically, often as a result of public pressure. For example, it is no longer acceptable for zoos to have a single representative of an animal species in a barred cage or, more recently, for an aquarium to train killer whales to perform circus-like acts in a pool. Less dramatically in the museum context, amassing a collection simply for the sake of amassing a collection is an indicator of institutional self-absorption. A human history museum can use its collection simply to display and identify the material output of a chapter in history, or it can endeavour to interpret that chapter in its prevailing social context. A natural history museum can display the fossil record of ancient life with or without mention of rapid, human-caused rates of declining biodiversity and increasing extinction. A science centre may not be presenting to its visitors any of the major science and technology issues that are pertinent to its region. A museum can simply open its doors to its traditional audience, or it can actively try to engage a broader audience with its resources. Museums of all kinds have choices, choices that characterize them as being negative, neutral, or positive influences with respect to the needs of humanity and this planet.

A strong adjunct to the rise in social responsibility has been the recently advancing notion of social entrepreneurship. In 1995, Harvard University's Kennedy School of Government published a synthesis of its two decades of research and reflection on creating public value in government (Moore 1998). One of the next major contributions to the field was the notion that socially responsible non-profits could "profit" by partnering with like-minded commercial corporations (Steckel, Simons, Simons & Tanen 1999).

Next came a new series of publications in the field of social entrepreneurship. In 1998, the National Center for Nonprofit Boards in the United

States issued an informative pamphlet about merging mission and money (Boschee 1998), followed by a special issue of its periodical on the topic (U.S. National Center for Nonprofit Boards 2001a). Then in 2001, a team at Stanford University published a benchmark synthesis on its three years of work about social entrepreneurship (Dees, Emerson & Economy 2001). Placing a greater emphasis on creating social value than on how much profit is made, this team proposed that social entrepreneurs act as agents of change in the following five sequential ways: 1) adopting a mission to create and sustain social value; 2) recognizing and relentlessly pursuing new opportunities to serve that mission; 3) engaging in a process of continuous innovation, adaptation, and learning; 4) acting boldly without being limited to resources in hand; and 5) exhibiting a heightened sense of accountability to the constituencies served and for the outcomes created.

There are close parallels between this course of action and what has transpired at Liberty Science Center. Specifically, our mission statement has a clear statement of "so what?" Faced with financial difficulties in our early years, then with new leadership who had been advocating John Cotton Dana's type of philosophy (Dana 1999) since the mid-'90s (Koster 1995), Liberty Science Center's mission was restated to be clearly orientated to the common good in human and environmental terms. We then had the conviction that we could significantly add, in a sustainable way, to Liberty Science Center's operating resources by contracting out with the state government for the innovative application of our educational programs to those who needed our resources most. In turn, this program has most definitely heightened our sense of accountability to the large underserved audience with whom we are now a major, interdependent partner.

We believe that there are, in turn, parallels of this situation to be found in all types of museum (Gurian 2002), especially those dedicated to finding new revenues from discerning sources. In terms of earned revenue, it is an axiom that the public votes with its feet. Following the trend in tourism, the world's largest industry, in which cultural and ecological reasons for travel now outweigh strictly recreational reasons, we think that the changing state of the world will increasingly make people seek more meaningful experiences about what is useful to know about the world. Although museums often regard attendance as a major performance parameter, with admission revenue among the main earned-revenue sources, it is unwise to equate popularity with external usefulness (Koster 1999) or individual enlightenment (Kimmelman 2001). In terms of contributed revenues, a pronounced trend is already clear. Driven by the movement towards social responsibility and a clear interest in tangible and useful outcomes, an increasing number of corporations, and already most foundations, are at a point of demanding that what they support has demonstrable benefits to society and/or the environment.

For museums, the optimal philosophy and practice therefore seem clear. For reasons of both usefulness and revenue, museums should indeed pursue a course of increased external consciousness. John Cotton Dana had an appropriate and beneficial vision for museums whose time seems to be now finally arriving: learn what the community needs, he advocated, and fit the museum to those needs. As earlier noted, for natural history museums – and here we would add zoos, aquariums and botanical gardens – it is also recognized nowadays that such institutions need to learn what the environment needs and fit the institution to those needs. If a museum still has the luxury of a more classical course of self-interest, its lifetime may well be finite, as public and contributor tastes change with the evolving atmosphere of the world in which we live.

ACKNOWLEDGMENTS

The first author wishes to thank Robert R. Janes and Janet Pieschel for their invitation to be a contributor at the session on social responsibility and museums at the 2002 conference of the Canadian Museums Association that has given rise to this book. In terms of the development of his philosophy about the social and environmental responsibility movement in museums, he also wishes to thank many colleagues at the Ontario Science Centre, Liberty Science Center, elsewhere in North America, and around the world for countless contributing conversations.

The second author wishes in particular to thank the many program colleagues at Liberty Science Center and many outside supporters who have played a pivotal role in enabling the development and success of the socially responsible initiatives that form the core of this article.

We are both deeply indebted to all of these colleagues. Collegiality, teamwork, and partnership are the lifeblood of museums, and we salute this way of working, one that we feel sure is the only way to make a positive difference in this world. In this regard, we also both wish to gratefully acknowledge the steadfast support of Liberty Science Center's Board of Trustees in the ongoing quest for new, more useful paradigms in what a museum does, and for whom. In particular, we recognize the Chair of the Board, Robert J. Dougherty, Jr., and Chair of its Science and Technology Committee, William A. Tansey, III, MD.

REFERENCES

American Association of Museums
    1984   *Museums for a new century: A report of the Commission on Museums for a New Century*. Washington, D.C.: American Association of Museums.
    1992   *Excellence and equity – Education and the public dimension of museums*. Washington, D.C.: American Association of Museums.
    2002   *Mastering civic engagement: A challenge to museums*. Washington, D.C.: American Association of Museums.

Barker, Richard
    2002   *On the nature of leadership*. Lanham, Maryland: University of America Press.

Barrett, Richard
    1998   *Liberating the corporate soul*. Boston: Butterworth-Heinemann.

Boschee, Jerr
    1998   *Merging mission with money*. Washington, D.C.: U.S. National Center for Nonprofit Boards.

Brousseau, Francine
    2003   True or false? *Muse*, 21, 23.

Carbonne, Stan
    2003   The dialogic museum. *Muse*, 21, 36–39.

Casey, Dawn
    2001   Museums as agents of social and political change. *Curator*, 44(3), 230–36.

Conservation Company
    2002   Evaluation of the Liberty Science Center tobacco education program, June 2002. Available from Liberty Science Center.

Covey, Stephen
    1990   *The seven habits of highly effective people: Powerful lessons in personal phange*. New York: Simon & Schuster.

Dana, John Cotton
    1999   *The new museum: Selected writings by John Cotton Dana*. Edited by William A. Peniston. Newark, N.J.: Newark Museum Association ; Washington, D.C.: American Association of Museums

Dees, Gregory, Emerson, Jed, and Economy, Peter
    2001   *Enterprising nonprofits: A toolkit for social entrepreneurs.* New York: John Wiley & Sons.

Falk, John
    1998   Visitors – who does, who doesn't, and why? *American Association of Museums Museum News* (March/April), 38–43.

Gurian, Elaine
    2002   Choosing among the options: an opinion about museum definitions. *Curator,* 45(2), 75–88.

Harvard University, John F. Kennedy School of Government
    2001   *Museums in the United States at the turn of the millennium: An industry note.* Conference of the U.S. Museums Trustee Association, Museum Governance in a New Age, October 4–7, 2001.

Kimmelman, Michael
    2001   Museums in a quandary: Where are the ideals? *The New York Times* (August 26).

King, Charles and Siegel, Michael
    2001   The master settlement agreement with the tobacco industry and cigarette advertising in magazines. *New England Journal of Medicine,* 345(7), 504–11.

Koster, Emlyn
    1995   The human journey and the evolving museum. In Michel Côté and Annette Viel (Eds.), Museums: Where knowledge is shared (pp. 81–98). Quebec City: Société des musées québécois and Musée de la civilisation.
    1999   In search of relevance – science centers as innovators in the evolution of museums. *Daedalus, Journal of the American Academy of Arts and Sciences,* 128, 277–96. (Issue devoted to *America's Museums,* Stephen Graubard, Ed.)
    2002   A tragedy revisited. *Muse,* 20, 26–27.

Leahy, Stephen
    2003   Greening stewardship. *Muse,* 21, 22–26.

Liberty Science Center
    2001   *The science behind tobacco.* www.lsc.org/tobacco.

Moore, Mark
    1998   *Creating public value: Strategic management in government.* Cambridge, Massachusetts: Harvard University Press.

Parston, Greg
    1997   Producing social results. In Frances Hesselbein, et al. (Eds.), *The Organization of the Future* (pp. 341–48). San Francisco: Jossey-Bass.

Peters, Tom and Waterman, Robert
    1982   *In search of excellence: Lessons from America's best-run companies.* New York: Harper & Row.

Schiele, Bernard and Koster, Emlyn
    2000   *Science centers in this century.* Sainte-Foy, Quebec: MultiMondes.

Smithsonian Institution
    1997   *Museums for the new millennium: A symposium for the museum community.* Proceedings of a conference commemorating the 150th anniversary of the Smithsonian Institution, 5–7 September 1996, Washington, D.C.: Center for Museum Studies/American Association of Museums.

Steckel, Richard, Simons, Robin, Simons, Jeffrey, and Tanen, Norman
    1999   *Making money while making a difference.* Homewood, Illinois: High Tide Press.

U.S. Centers for Disease Control
    2001   Monitoring the future study. University of Michigan, 2 November 2001.

U.S. Department of Health and Human Services
    2001   Substance abuse and mental health services administration. Summary findings from the 2000 National Household Survey on Drug Abuse.

U.S. National Center for Nonprofit Boards
    2001a   Profit potential: advancing your mission through social entrepreneurship. *Board Member,* 10(5), 1–15.
    2001b   Mission accomplished: The board's role in outcome measurement, *Board Member,* 10(8), 1–15. U.S. National Center for Nonprofit Boards

Weil, Stephen E.
    1999   Introduction. In Dana, John Cotton, *The new museum: Selected Writings by John Cotton Dana.* Edited by William A. Peniston. Newark, N.J.: Newark Museum Association; Washington, D.C.: American Association of Museums
    2002   *Making museums matter.* Washington, D.C.: Smithsonian Institution Press.

Worldwatch Institute
    2003   *State of the world 2003 – Special 20th anniversary edition.* New York: W.W. Norton and Company.

Worts, Douglas
    In press On the brink of irrelevance? Art museums in contemporary society. In Les Tickle et al. (Eds.) *Opening up the Cases: Visual Arts Education in Museums and Galleries.* Dordrecht: Kluwer

IS ART GOOD FOR YOU?

Susan Pointe

THE MCMULLEN ART GALLERY, UNIVERSITY OF ALBERTA HOSPITAL

Since at least the fifteenth century, hospitals in Europe have purchased and commissioned original artwork to improve the aesthetics of their sterile halls and cold, vacant public spaces (Staricoff & Duncan 2001). Today, several hospitals in the U.S. and Canada, as well as in Europe, can boast of possessing reputable collections of international artwork, some with over fifteen hundred works.

The McMullen Art Gallery, located within the University of Alberta Hospital in Edmonton, Alberta, Canada, looks and behaves like other not-for-profit art galleries in North America. In 1997 and 1998, however, the McMullen was becoming more and more irrelevant in the eyes of hospital staff, and was heading down the fatal path of closure.

As a result of reflecting on the needs of the gallery's local community, and the creation of a novel outreach program, the McMullen now faces a much brighter future.

One of only a handful of hospital art galleries in North America, the McMullen Art Gallery was planned at the same time that the University Hospital was undergoing a large expansion in 1986. Today, the hospital is one of the largest in Canada, with 306,570 square metres and 7,800 staff who serve 322,986 outpatients and 22,832 inpatients per year.

The integration of a gallery into the main floor plans of the new hospital was pushed through by hospital board member William McMullen. An avid art collector, McMullen believed that art should be where there is hurt and healing. At the same time, the hospital was already amassing a relatively large collection of artwork in the belief that art would humanize an otherwise architecturally cold institution. Today, the collection surpasses eleven hundred works.

Purpose-built to exhibit art, the gallery is open to the general public, hospital patients, visitors and staff, and admission is free. Despite the gallery's relatively small size of ninety-three square metres, it received seventeen thousand visitors in 2001, an extremely high attendance relative to other city galleries of the same size. This high attendance is due to the population of the hospital, as well as the location of the hospital in the centre of the University of Alberta campus. The gallery's public hours are also generous – from 10 a.m. to 8 p.m. Monday to Friday, and from 1 to 8 p.m. on Saturday and Sunday.

The main floor of the hospital was designed to mimic intersecting streetscapes, and is capped by a glass ceiling ten stories high on each wing. The main floor also serves as a major thoroughfare in the centre of the University of Alberta campus. The gallery is located on the main floor of the hospital, and is fronted by floor-to-ceiling windows, making it well situated for walk-in traffic. The McMullen looks and feels like an art gallery, however, and therefore attracts the same positive and negative public perceptions as do other art galleries and museums.

My position as Art Advisor is financially supported by the Friends of the University Hospital, and includes the responsibility of directing both the McMullen Art Gallery and the hospital's art collection. The Friends is the volunteer management agency for the hospital, with over six hundred volunteers, and also manages a very profitable hospital gift shop. With these gift shop revenues, the Friends support the Director of the Friends, three volunteer administration staff, four gift shop staff, the gallery's operating budget, the art collection, two full-time gallery staff (including the author) and seven part-time artists, in addition to providing an annual gift of $250,000 to the hospital.

Although the gallery was purpose-built to exhibit art, under the Friends' direction it was intended to be more than an art gallery. The gallery would also serve as a patient comfort zone, to encourage patient well-being by providing an environment that celebrates hope, compassion, beauty, creativity, and life.

I accepted the position of Art Advisor in 1999. At that time, I was in Toronto, so before I accepted the offer, I contacted a number of individuals in the Edmonton art community. Their feedback was extremely positive, indicating that the McMullen was a great space, hosted an excellent exhibition program, and had a very good reputation. The gallery maintained steady attendance at ten thousand visitors per year. On a superficial review, the McMullen had a very good reputation within the art community.

When I arrived at the hospital in January of 1999, several things became very clear in a matter of weeks. Although the gallery was mandated to serve patients, only 4 per cent of its visitors were hospital patients. Most patients did not know there was a gallery in the hospital, and many could not visit the main floor due to illness or physical limitations. Just as dismal was the staff attendance, at 15 per cent. Most hospital staff did not visit the gallery and many did not know why it was there; some had actually never heard of it.

To add to my growing concern, the chief executive officer of the hospital had little regard for art, let alone the gallery, and our statistics did not help. Like many institutions these days, the hospital was extremely stretched for space, and the gallery was sitting on a prime revenue-generating location. A number of for-profit ventures could easily replace the gallery, and provide much-needed revenues to the hospital. To further my distress, I overheard a devastating comment which ensured that something had to be done: as I was leaving the gallery one day, a third-year medical student was touring a group of first-year medical students through the hospital. He stopped in front of the gallery and said, "This is the art gallery, and I have no idea why it is here." The group walked on.

On any given day, ten thousand patients, staff and visitors walk through the hospital doors. This is the size of a small town, yet only 19 per cent of our visitors came from the hospital. Indeed, while the art community might have been satisfied with the McMullen's programming, the gallery was clearly not seen to be relevant or interesting by patients and staff. We had some work to do.

Although we felt we knew some of the causes of this poor attendance, such as a lack of awareness, we also knew that we needed to confirm our suspicions by conducting interviews with any staff member who would make the time. In these interviews, we did not question our mandate, but rather explored staff and patient needs. We also explored where and what type of art programming could fulfil those needs, and in the process, we discovered several opportunities.

Contrary to a popular myth, not all patients are "in and out" of the hospital, particularly in an acute care hospital such as the University of Alberta's. Transplant, burn, infectious disease and tuberculosis patients can remain hospitalized for up to eight months, and these adult patients have little but television and magazines to pass their time. Forty-three per cent of our patients were also from outside the Edmonton region, and their visitors were few. As a consequence, patient boredom was a leading issue for nursing staff. Boredom intensifies a patient's pain, fear, anxiety, and depression, which then find expression in other physical illnesses.

As a result of the interviews, we concluded that we could address both the threat to the gallery, and patient and staff needs, through an awareness campaign and new program design. First, we dealt with awareness. This was addressed by creating signage, and lots of it. Today, every hospital room, waiting room, hallway and elevator has signage, including a message about why the gallery exists.

Second, we examined our exhibition content. The hospital's art collection was permanently installed in patient rooms, clinics and public areas. While the gallery had been selecting exhibitions from the Edmonton art community, whose media, content and themes appealed to a diversity of interests, we chose to open up our exhibition call to the larger community, including the heritage and museum community in Alberta and across Canada. If necessary, we assist each group with funding.

Third, we addressed the gallery's "uninviting atmosphere." Despite the fire regulations, we opened our double doors to the gallery and kept them open. We then designed a Drop-In Studio program on every Thursday from 2 to 5 p.m., open to all visitors. At the Drop-In Studio, patients, visitors, staff and members of the public can try their hand at painting, drawing, printmaking, sculpture, and so on. We created a large fluorescent green banner, hanging in the hospital's main corridor, which reads,

"McMullen Gallery for Patients, Staff, and Visitors, Drop-In Studio EVERY Thursday from 2 to 5."

In addition, we threw out our comment book, which seemed only to invite comments like "nice show," "Smith's artwork is beautiful" and "beautiful gallery." Comments like these had done little to convince the hospital's administration of our relevance. Instead, we designed a feedback card on which we articulated our mandate and invited visitors to let us know if we achieved it. In one exhibition, we placed our mission statement on the wall and invited our visitors to write feedback on the wall in response.

Ultimately, program design and location were the most challenging initiatives, but also the most rewarding. As stated earlier, many of the University of Alberta Hospital patients could not visit the gallery because of the severity of their illnesses, or the supervision required for the support machinery they required. As a result, we had to design a program that could go beyond the gallery walls and attract attention. If patients and staff could not, or would not, visit then we would go to them.

THE ARTISTS-ON-THE-WARDS PROGRAM

It did not take extensive research to discover several American hospitals were pushing their art programming beyond hanging artwork on hospital walls (Samuels & Rockwood Lane 1998). These hospitals hired artists, known as artists-on-the-wards, to work one-on-one at the bedsides of child and adult patients. Patients could try their hand at painting, sculpture, writing poetry, theatre and dance, with the guidance of a practising artist. At their simplest, these artist-led activities were offered to patients as diversion and entertainment. At their most profound level, medical staff members were noting, and publishing, that creative experiences enhanced patients' healing (McLoed 1996).

In October of 1999, the Director of the Friends and I conducted a study tour of the Shands Medical Center in Gainesville, Florida, the most prominent artists-on-the-wards program in the United States. We returned home with a program model that we could implement. Since 75 per cent of the University of Alberta Hospital patients were adults, and since the young patients had a fair amount of recreational programming in place,

The McMullen Art Gallery takes art to the patients on the wards.

we chose to target the hospital's adult population. For the pilot project, we selected four areas of patient care, including cardiology, pulmonary, cardio-thoracic, and eating disorders. We also chose three visual artists to lead the way, each of whom would work eight hours per week for six months, after being trained on each unit.

As you can imagine, the impact of working with visual artists was immediately visible. The artists moved through the hospital wearing blue aprons and pushing their art carts, and you could not miss them. If the patients were physically unable to paint, the artists would paint for them – often painting the windows of the patient's room or creating compositions for them to keep. The hospital units selected for the pilot project were immediately transformed with colourful painterly images. For those patients willing and able, the artists led them in the creation of "Murals of Hands." These murals were full of hands traced by patients, and then decorated with line, shape and texture, or words of hope, love and anger – whatever the patient wished. These murals were then installed on the units and added to over the next year. These murals are not only powerful to look at, but are also physical tributes to the patients who had stayed at the hospital. We were surprised at how important these murals became for the staff, as remembrances of those patients.

The artists also led patients in the creation of "Healing Tiles" and a "Healing Ceiling," where patients painted 6 by 6-inch ceramic tiles. The more ambitious patients would paint on 16 by 16-inch ceiling tiles, which were then installed in the ceilings of their hospital units. With these projects, we witnessed the creative spirit emerge. Patients expressed their individuality and identity, while hopefully regaining a little dignity within the hospital context. Perhaps most importantly, we observed how much patients enjoyed being with the artists, recapturing feelings of joy, happiness and humour.

Staff and family members were also invited to paint tiles, and many responded. It was always very moving to see how the simple act of painting a tile for someone who was terminally ill was so important for the families of these patients, including the nursing staff. At times, a patient's tile would be their last creative act. Naturally, these tiles are particularly special to the patients' families and our program, and they are treated as such.

Verbal and written feedback of the program from patients, nursing and medical staff was immediate, and overwhelmingly positive. In staff evaluations of the program, one nursing staff member wrote:

> The times that we have observed the artist with the patients, the mood of the patients seems to be brighter. The patients have something to do and this may lessen the amount of depression they may experience because of their surgery…. The patients also seem more motivated and determined to ambulate or get involved in returning to daily activities. (Briones, personal communication 2000)

Another staff member wrote:

> Since these wonderful teams of artists have joined the rest of the medical team, there appears to be less stress and anxiety with the patients. The change is almost immediate and you can see a new glow in the patient's face. (Tsounis, personal communication 2000)

Shortly after the visual artists began work, the Alberta Foundation for the Arts awarded the Friends of the University Hospital a Community Project Grant. With this additional funding, we expanded the pilot project to include two poet/writers. The poets would read to the patients, guide patients in their own writing, or translate patients' reminiscences into poetry. The poets also left evidence of their own presence, writing poems or quotations on unit whiteboards and windows, or leaving them for staff at the unit desk. The poets also created installations, such as the "Hope Tree," a life-size tree painted on one of the large unit windows. Patients, staff, and visitors were then invited to write positive affirmations onto pre-cut leaves and paste them onto the tree. Within two weeks, the tree was absolutely full. The poets also created installations of the patients' writing, and we are currently installing "The Poets Walk" on our very busy second-floor corridor. Fifteen patients have allowed us to frame and permanently display their poems there. Cut in vinyl lettering, and interwoven between each frame, is a poem about the healing nature of writing.

After his wife's death in the hospital, a gentleman wrote a thank-you note to one of our poets. It read:

> I want to thank you for your great kindness to my Sofia during her long and horrible ordeal.... I am sure you noted the warm and radiant smile with which she greeted you.... Your visits meant much to her. The words you have written give me solace, and were enormously appreciated by both Sofia and me. Thank-you, they are now treasured mementos of a difficult end, and tragic time.... The hospital is made more tolerable by your happy presence. (Personal and confidential communication, July 13, 2000).

Over the year, it is not surprising that the poets collected many poems written by patients. In order to celebrate these individuals, they put together an anthology titled, "Read Two Poems and Call Me in the Morning," and had it professionally printed. Like the tile projects, the anthology unveils the patients as brave heroes and profoundly interesting individuals with limitless strength. Their poems are courageous and raw, and have a very powerful effect on the reader.

Pulmonologist Dr. Dale Lein wrote:

> For patients in the hospital, this is typically a time when they are under a great deal of stress, very anxious about their lives. The interaction with the artists seems to give them a sense of control, purpose and accomplishment that brings balance back to many of them. Clearly physical healing is only one aspect of well-being and I think your program plays a significant role in the psychological healing associated with disease. I would like to offer my whole-hearted support and hope that your program will continue indefinitely. (Lein, personal communication 2000)

Just as we were completing our second year, we began to receive unsolicited media attention from local newspapers, television stations and a national magazine. The Friends' Board of Directors was very pleased with the response to the program, and indicated that they would continue to support the work indefinitely. This support was further increased by another grant from the Alberta Foundation for the Arts, which was also pleased with the media attention and the growing profile of the program.

At the same time, the Canadian Millennium Partnership Program awarded the Friends organization a one-time grant to expand the project. This allowed us to add two musicians, one dancer and one theatre artist, resulting in the creation of a multidisciplinary team. With this team of seven artists, we were able to increase our coverage of hospital units to include tuberculosis, infectious diseases, trauma, general surgery, nephrology, neurology, burns, as well as dialysis and medical outpatients. At this point, our team was visiting thirty nursing units.

IS THIS PROGRAM ART THERAPY?

One issue that merits discussion at this point is the difference between the Artists-on-the-Wards program and art therapy. Art therapy is a licenced, master's-level specialty, with its foundations in psychology and psychotherapy. Art therapists are clinical practitioners and therapists. They use art as a tool to access unspoken emotions, as well as to analyze, diagnose, and interpret a patient's psychological profile. The Artists-on-the-Wards program is not art therapy, as it provides patients with the opportunity to work with an artist and to make art, and not be in any kind of therapy.

Nevertheless, some art therapists are artists, and as artists, they lead creative activities at the patient's bedside as part of their practice. It is important to note that each program has its own power. At the Shands Medical Center, both an art therapy program and an artists-on-the-wards program coexist and complement each other in their approaches. My hope is that we will see both of these programs develop in all types of Canadian hospitals.

REFLECTING ON OUR DIRECTIONS

Unlike some hospitals in the U.S., I do not have any miraculous stories to prove that invoking the creative spirit will save lives. Those stories will come when the patients are ready to share them, and our program is still relatively young. My purpose here is to share the details of an outreach program, which appears to fit the needs of our primary community. Now approaching its fourth year, the Artists-on-the-Wards program has funding and a life of its own.

In 1999, the University of Alberta Hospital had almost given up on the vision that an art gallery space was useful. They questioned who used it and why it was there. As we designed and installed the Artists-on-the-Wards program, I continued to be very concerned about the fate of the gallery. Technically, the Artists-on-the-Wards program does not rely on the physical existence of the gallery, since it is delivered at the patient's bedside. We knew, however, that the Artists-on-the-Wards program would generate increased awareness of the gallery, but we did not anticipate how much.

The overall annual attendance for the gallery increased 40 per cent from 1998 to 2001. The percentage of patient visitors increased from 4 to 22 per cent, while staff visitation rose from 15 to 46 per cent. More family members of patients began to use the gallery as a place to wait while patients were in surgery, getting tests, and meeting with medical staff. One of our patients stated:

> Thank you for providing such a healing place in my traumatic time. After being poked and prodded, I come here to calm down before I leave the hospital to face the rest of life ... I know now, for me, it will be a part of my healing. (Anonymous communication, May 1999)

Another patient wrote:

> It [the gallery] is a place of peace and renewal for me. I first discovered the gallery when my son lay deathly ill upstairs. It was a place of refuge and sanctuary.... (Anonymous communication, November 2001)

Finally, we were receiving the statistics and quotable feedback we needed to take to the hospital's CEO. This proved to be unnecessary, however, as the CEO had remained abreast of all of our endeavours to become more relevant to the hospital, and neither she nor her staff questioned the relevance of the gallery. The last hospital-wide space evaluation, in which every square metre is re-examined for more efficient use by a team of diverse staff, stated: "The McMullen Gallery is a precious and rare space in this type of environment. Every effort should be made to conserve and enhance it" (Capital Health Authority 2001).

This article is written from the perspective of one manager of a small, not-for-profit gallery, and I accept responsibility for the biases I have developed over the course of my experience. At the same time, there are lessons to be learned and shared from the experience we have had in the last four years. In short, when faced with the potential closure of the McMullen Gallery, we saw an opportunity to rethink and redesign our programs in a way that was truer to our mandate, and considerably more sensitive to our community's needs.

ARE WE REALLY IN THE BUSINESS OF EXHIBITS?

How often do we see a museum or gallery reduce or eliminate their outreach programs when faced with fiscal restraints? Yet, these fiscal restraints are often the result of communities, and their politicians, questioning the social relevance of the museum.

The McMullen Gallery was fortunate. Unlike most other city, provincial, and national galleries, the McMullen does not exist "to collect and conserve." Mandated by the Friends and the University of Alberta Hospital to be a patient comfort zone, the number-one priority of the McMullen is to serve hospital patients. Because of this, we were able to reorient our staffing and operating budget to address our patients' needs, without going through a philosophical debate about our primary purpose. If a museum or gallery places its institutional priority on collecting and conserving, rather than educating or meeting community needs, I believe it will continue to struggle when faced with concerns about social relevance.

It was our outreach program, rather than our exhibitions, that motivated and inspired our most influential community, the patients and the hospital staff. It was no coincidence that, when the Artists-on-the-Wards program was implemented, our attendance began to rise. In addition, the gallery was seen as the birthplace of the Artists-on-the-Wards program, and thus staff and patients soon recognized that the gallery was more than a traditional art gallery. I also suspect that, although some staff and patients will still not visit the gallery, they would lobby against any threat to its presence within the hospital. The reason is simple: they enjoy the outreach programming.

YOU GET WHAT YOU PAY FOR

When we hire staff, it is important to remember that we get what we pay for. Like many museums and galleries, our gallery uses a combination of paid staff and volunteers to meet the demand of the Artists-on-the-Wards programs. We have a budget to hire seven part-time positions, and setting the hourly wage for these positions was the most difficult challenge we faced. Much debate surrounded it. It may not be a surprise that the Friends were very resistant to paying the artists at all. They expected the program to be facilitated exclusively by volunteers, and some Board members still believe this. We were confronted with this ideological stance for three reasons. First, I was developing the program under a volunteer-management agency. Second, other hospital "arts and crafts" programs were run by volunteers, and third, museums and galleries are notorious for underpaying their educators. Many educators are volunteers!

Fortunately, we were able to set the wage at a competitive rate, comparable to better-paying teaching positions in larger galleries. Because of this, we were able to demand high skill levels and expect a minimum commitment of a year. This combination of the artists' high skill levels, and their consistency as staff, ensured the success of the program.

We also sought artists who were formally trained and practising their craft at least part-time, with a minimum of three years of adult teaching experience. We looked for experience in health care, demonstrated empathy and sensitivity towards others, and a maturity level that would indicate an ability to appropriately handle serious patient discussions. The artists we selected not only met the above requirements, but also held graduate degrees in their discipline. They had considerable teaching experience, particularly at the college level, and had the maturity and skill to interact effectively with health-care staff of all ages and specialties. Our artists' teaching experience and superior facilitation skills have been critically important in engaging adult patients. Again, due to their skill level and maturity, our artists have not only worked at the bedside, but they have also assisted us in making presentations and leading workshops for medical staff.

In most large museums and galleries, educators and program staff are typically responsible for leading learning activities in the schools, in the community, and in the galleries. They are the public face of the museum. It is also the education staff who hear most of the visitor feedback, simply because of their public responsibilities within the museum. Yet, due to institutional priority or budget allocation, the education staff are some of the lowest paid staff, or are volunteers. In addition, some museums and galleries are further blinded by professional biases, hiring art historians or artists to fill education positions. Instead, they should be seeking evidence of superior teaching and facilitation skills, as a good art historian or talented artist does not necessarily make a good art instructor. Art galleries, in particular, have an opportunity to be the centres of the best in art education. With the education system in Canada cutting back on its art programs, galleries have a wonderful opportunity to link the public with some of the best art educators available.

NEVER UNDERESTIMATE THE POWER OF HANDS-ON EXPERIENCE

Other educators have stated this axiom before: do not underestimate the power of working with artists or watching artists work. For years, art advocates have argued that displaying art offers patients many benefits. However, when our patients began to create poems, paintings, and songs, the response was electric and supports what I have always believed. A hands-on experience with an art form is very powerful, and I challenge other art galleries and museums to increase the quality of their current hands-on programs. I also challenge them to create high-quality, hands-on programs for adults as well as for children.

Unfortunately, anecdotal evidence from the letters and evaluations of patients and staff are not enough to prove to medical administration that fostering creativity in patients has value. The need for a well-designed and thorough study of our program intensifies each year. To satisfy the questions of the medical community, we will ultimately have to study the physiological effects of fostering creativity in patients, including a number of factors such as blood pressure, pain control and tumour response. I believe that the longevity of our program in the hospital rests on our ability to undertake such studies, and to demonstrate the outcomes to support our claims.

WHO ARE YOUR MOST IMPORTANT STAKEHOLDERS?

One of the first lessons we learned was to identify our stakeholders, and to know their order of importance. Prior to 1999, the McMullen Gallery was communicating in a way that suggested that the art community was the most important stakeholder. The former gallery manager believed this to be the case, along with holding the conviction that a gallery with a good exhibition program would prevail. For the art community, the gallery was behaving like a traditional art gallery, and was effective. Once we decided that staff and patients were our most important stakeholders, the program design was straightforward. We built our program in response to staff and patient need.

Keeping your stakeholders happy can be a juggling act. We know this, and need to get on with it, but many museums and galleries assume that it is their *exhibitions* that will help or hurt them. I wonder how many museums use this as an excuse not to respond to an obvious need in their communities. I continue to believe that high-quality outreach programs, which respond to community needs, can be very effective in gaining attendance, members, donations, sponsorship, and overall community support. I am not suggesting that a museum sacrifice quality in their exhibitions; rather, I am suggesting that outreach programming may be as important as exhibitions. For museums seeking social relevance, they will need to explore this and make it an institutional priority.

DO WE NEED A MUSEUM AT ALL?

There is still one issue that challenges me, which I mentioned at the beginning of this article. In an acute-care hospital, the majority of the patients are too ill or too "hooked up" to visit the gallery. If they do, many require assistance to visit. Given this challenge, would our money be better spent on temporary art exhibitions throughout the hospital, rather than on a gallery which many of our community members cannot visit? Is a physical space essential to the work we are mandated to do? For many galleries, the answer is a resounding "yes"; for others it may be "no."

I leave this question for readers to ponder. When you start to explore the needs of your community, and your ability to address those needs, the answers may threaten the very existence of your museum. Ironically, this is an exercise upon which the museum's survival may depend.

REFERENCES

Capital Health Authority
    2001   Capital health authority master plan. Revised 2001. Edmonton: Capital Health Authority.

McLoed, M.
    1996   RX: A dose of creativity. *High Performance* (Winter), 17–21.

Samuels, M. and Rockwood Lane, M.
    1998   *Creative healing: How to heal yourself by tapping your hidden creativity.* San Francisco: Harper.

Staricoff, R.L. and Duncan, J.A.
    2001   *A Study of the Effects of the Visual and Performing Arts in Healthcare* (report). London: Chelsea Westminster Hospital.

NEGOTIATING A SUSTAINABLE PATH: MUSEUMS AND SOCIETAL THERAPY

Glenn C. Sutter and Douglas Worts

DEFINING BASIC ISSUES

How can more than six billion people lead peaceful and fulfilling lives on a planet that has a limited ability to meet our needs and wants? This question has sparked countless debates and actions aimed at sustainability, where different forms of development are supposed to "meet the needs of the present without compromising the ability of future generations to meet their own needs."[1] Debates about water, endangered species, social justice, biotechnology, militarism, and, most recently, the Kyoto Protocol, have kept aspects of sustainability in the public eye, and there is growing concern about forms of economic development that have undesirable social and ecological impacts. But trying to respond to all of these problems in isolation is not likely to produce a desirable future. Values and patterns of behaviour from the past are being transformed as new pressures from globalization are creating opportunities and challenges that humanity has not faced before. Increased consciousness, along with a revised set of values, will be necessary if our various societies are to share and consume resources in an equitable and sustainable way.

The challenge we face is a cultural one, since "development divorced from its human or cultural context is growth without a soul" (UNESCO 1995). While our lives are shaped by the decisions we make and the things we do as individuals and groups, the cultural values that support our choices and actions will ultimately determine whether our societies will be sustainable or not. The problem is that people are often reluctant to acknowledge the significance and impacts of their choices and actions, let alone the cultural values that support them. People with economic and political power, especially in the West, are worried about the consequences of a fundamental shift in our lifestyles. Some leaders are trying to figure out how better to distribute wealth in an increasingly globalized world, where the "haves" traditionally depend on the "have-nots." Others want to protect their corner of it and preserve the status quo. Industries, businesses, nations, communities, religions, and individuals are all experiencing this scramble, and have been slow to respond because change always starts a domino reaction – and that, for many, is scary. Yet, since sustainable development became an international standard with the publication of the Brundtland report *Our Common Future* (United Nations 1987), the number of organizations that claim to be active in this area has grown tremendously, and this trend is likely to continue for some time. Unlike some debates and the uncertainties that spark them, the need for sustainable forms of development shows no signs of fading away. Unfortunately, there are few indications that we are effecting real changes in our lifestyles and moving closer to a sustainable path.

In this article, we describe sustainability as a path, and suggest that society needs therapy. We chose to call sustainability a "path," as opposed to a "destination," because while it has elements of both, the distinction is important. Defining sustainability as a destination reflects linear thinking, where society has to pass a series of milestones in order to reach some distant location. This approach to development is a common feature of Western industrialized cultures, but it has limited value when applied to sustainability. It is more appropriate to consider the dynamic nature of social and ecological systems and define sustainability as a social, environmental, economic, and spiritual trajectory that not only has to be developed (or rediscovered) but constantly reinforced. This is more in keeping with the realities of cultural development, where changes may be understandable and measurable but are often chaotic. At the same time, defining and staying on this sort of path requires a repeating and integrated series of checks and balances, as opposed to dealing with issues (like climate change) in isolation.

The museum community is increasingly interested in sustainability,[2] which is definitely a good sign. But there is a growing "sustainability" bandwagon that tries to argue that museums should be sustained as they currently are. Their argument is typically based on the old rhetoric of how undeniably good museums are – and that they should be better supported. Other museologists would rather reshape museums so that they effectively contribute to society's overall sustainability. Presented with challenges ranging from a growing ecological crisis, systemic social inequities, skyrocketing urbanization, and the increasing complexity of culturally pluralistic communities, they see an opportunity for museums to play new, catalytic, and galvanizing roles. If this were actually achieved, instead of the current preoccupation with museums as cultural tourism-engines, then there would be compelling reasons for continued or increased public funding.

For the authors of this article and others in the museum community, sustainability involves revisiting the first principles of museum work, assessing the cultural needs and opportunities of our communities, and evaluating how our institutions are engaging and addressing those cultural situations. We believe that, while museums can and should be addressing sustainability through the non-formal education system, they also have a much broader role to play as active facilitators of social change at local and regional levels. Our motivation reflects the fact that sustainability requires a focus on complex, dynamic systems, the development of an ecocentric world view (Rowe 1992, Sutter 2001), an appreciation for how we understand our underlying values, and shifts in how consciously held values are reflected in our daily lives. Our thinking has also been influenced by the development of *The Human Factor* exhibit at the Royal Saskatchewan Museum, and by activities of the Working Group on Museums and Sustainable Communities, coordinated by the Canadian Museum of Nature.[3]

The intent of this article is to explore the links between sustainability (in the Brundtland sense), culture, and the potential of museums as agents of social change. We consider issues around sustainability and unsustainability to be cultural matters, where culture involves the myriad ways in which people relate to their world. We see culture resting on, and responding to, the complex set of values and actions that link individuals and groups to their ecosystems – much of which remain beyond their control and understanding (Worts 2003). Many cultures in the "developing world" are trying to meet the basic human needs of their citizens, often by emulating Western lifestyles that offer wealth and security. The challenges facing the industrialized or "developed" world have more to do with consciousness, relatedness, and humility.

Given that sustainability is a relatively new concept in museum circles, we start with an overview of the topic, including why society needs "therapy." We then describe how *The Human Factor* was developed as an attempt to address sustainability from an exhibit perspective. In the last section, we elaborate on four key points about the role that museums might play in creating a culture of sustainability.

THE SUSTAINABILITY CHALLENGE

To be sustainable, human activities have to be conducted with respect to ecological principles, including the fact that ecosystems have limits. For example, from small puddles to the global ecosphere, every ecosystem has a carrying capacity defined by the maximum number of organisms it can support. If a population exceeds this maximum, corrective measures such as dispersal or increased mortality due to disease will eventually cause it to fall below carrying capacity. Humans have managed to increase their global carrying capacity in the past by developing new technologies, notably in agriculture and medicine, but we are ultimately constrained by ecological limitations.

Whether or not we appreciate ecological limits is another matter. Despite clear evidence that our impacts are causing ecological stress – the Antarctic ozone hole and the shrinking Aral Sea are prime examples – we are hesitant to question underlying actions and values. We continue to insist that all types of progress are desirable, and that human economies can expand beyond a level that ecosystems can support. We stand amazed at the riches produced by compound interest, seeing it as a path to fortune, forgetting that exponential growth is also a feature of cancer and pyramid schemes. Similarly, people are reluctant to acknowledge that actions taken by a small number of us can now have global consequences, both positive and negative.

The goal of any sustainable development is to maintain the health of social and ecological systems so that all stakeholders have a fair opportunity to live a fulfilling life. To achieve this at the cultural level, people need to be more conscious of their social and ecological relationships. We also need to foster a sense of individual and collective responsibility for both ourselves and the others who share this planet. One of the largest challenges we face is developing adequate feedback about the consequences of our choices. Anyone reading these words is likely living an unsustainable lifestyle – despite our efforts to avoid this state. The question is: how do we know where we are in the sustainability challenge?

Sustainability indicators do exist, but they are far from complete or sufficient. One powerful indicator is the ecological footprint, which measures the productive land and water needed to support a person or population at a given standard of living. Ecological footprints are estimates of the area needed both to produce the materials we consume and to turn our wastes back into productive elements in the ecosystem (Wackernagel & Rees 1995). They indicate that human activities have reached a point that the global ecosystem cannot sustain.[4]

A second line of evidence comes from an alternative measure of economic health called the Genuine Progress Indicator (GPI),[5] which has been used to highlight the limitations of the more traditional Gross Domestic Product (GDP).[6] The GPI suggests that the health of the U.S. economy was improving until the mid-1970s, and has been level or falling slightly ever since, presumably because of accumulating damage to social and ecological systems at the regional and global level (Cobb, Glickman & Chelog 2001).

The underlying pressure on these systems is a combination of values and attitudes that dominate in the industrialized world, powerful technologies, economic affluence, and a burgeoning world population. According to United Nations estimates,[7] the growth rate of the global population started to fall in the 1990s, but the total number of people is still rising, especially in low-income areas. Models suggest that world population will either peak at eight billion around 2040 and then decline to less than six billion, or it will grow to eighteen billion by the end of the twenty-first century.

Cast in this light, sustainability becomes a fundamental, cross-cutting, and elusive challenge that has already started to affect museums and the societies they reflect. It is fundamental because it not only reflects and responds to our personal and collective values, it also applies to all of our institutions, our daily decisions, and possibly the long-term survival of our species. It is cross-cutting because it involves processes and interactions that span or supersede political, institutional, and academic boundaries. And it is elusive partly because the social and ecological systems involved are highly variable, and often chaotic.

The classic model of sustainable development calls for an integration of social, economic, and environmental concerns, and is generally illustrated by three overlapping circles labelled "society," "economy," and "environment" (Worts 2003). In social terms, sustainability hinges on social justice, both locally and globally. Individuals need to feel that they are equal partners, as opposed to pawns, in the stewardship of human life. If equity is not achieved, the "have-nots" will not be motivated to contribute, and are likely to exacerbate problems by sheer weight of their numbers. This goes beyond a levelling of the economic playing field, and calls for a wholesale reduction in underlying prejudices and hatreds. From an economic perspective, sustainability requires the development of a steady-state economy (Daly 1999), where people live off the "interest" generated by social and ecological systems and avoid depleting stocks of natural, human, social, and manufactured capital.[8] In environmental or ecological terms, sustainability is about interactions, carrying capacity, and how systems recover from disturbance. Defined by flows of material and information, social and ecological systems cycle between different states based on the distribution and movement of capital (Holling 1992), and the rate of cycling depends on their innate resilience and feedbacks that can be positive or negative (Marten 2001). While human actions can affect the rate of cycling, sustainability is not about holding a social or ecological system in a given state, since this is impossible. The aim is to ensure that transitions from one state to another occur without reducing the potential welfare of future generations.

The three-circles model of sustainability has been justifiably criticized for a number of reasons (Worts 2003). One of its biggest drawbacks is that it suggests that human society and the world economy are equivalent to the global ecosystem, when they are actually subsets of it. A more realistic version (Fig. 1) indicates that any manifestation of human activity, such as a sustainable community, is ultimately supported and constrained by larger ecosystems. But the central point of both models – that social and ecological systems are inextricably linked – is widely accepted and

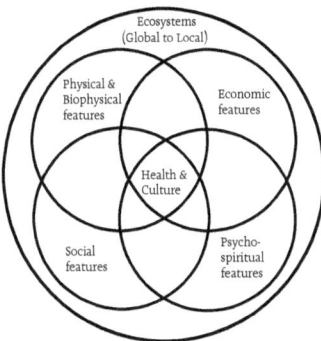

Figure 1. Aspects of a sustainable community. Note that all features interact to support derived qualities, such as health and culture, and that the community as a whole is constrained by ecosystems at various scales.

provides a foundation for elaborating on what sustainability actually means.

By defining sustainability in terms of economic development,[9] the Brundtland Commission challenged us to plan and act in ways that do not compromise the ability of future generations to meet their needs. Since then, the concept of sustainability has evolved into a way of thinking about the vitality and unpredictable behaviour of social and ecological systems, and a way of acting that limits the destruction or loss of natural, manufactured, social, and human capital. It can also be viewed as a pressure aimed at personal, institutional, and cultural development. In the end, sustainability requires an equal emphasis on ecosystem health, economic development, and social justice, because they are all mutually reinforcing (Marten 2001). It also requires humility, and an acknowledgment that humans are part of nature, with a capacity for consciousness that is invaluable and presumably unique, but often overlooked by contemporary society.

The notion that society needs therapy – or possibly full-blown analysis[10] – stems from recent work by ecological psychologists (e.g., Sheppard 1995, Winter 1996), who point out that unsustainable values and actions have their roots in the industrialized worldview. A major part of this worldview is a "human–nature split" that leads to social and physical isolation and may be preventing us from pursuing ecocentric forms of development (Fig. 2). Many types of isolation have been implicated, from physical barriers to schisms associated with academic and technical specialization. Historically, the human–nature split can be traced to philosophers such as Plato, Aristotle, and Augustine, who separated experiences of the mind from those of the body. The gap widened with

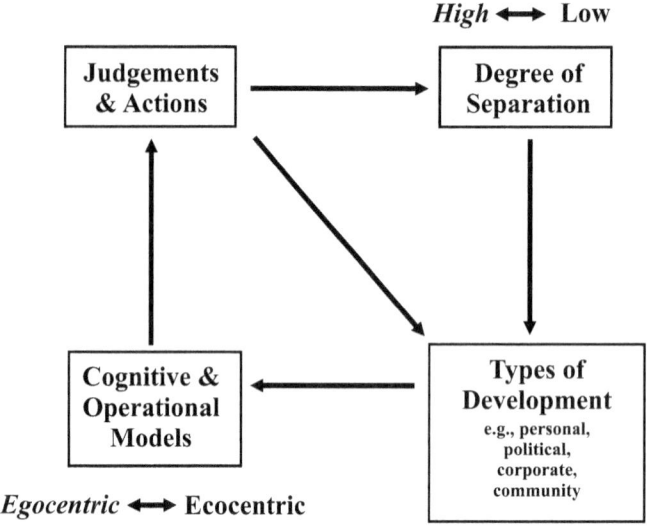

Figure 2. A generalized model illustrating how the human–nature split may be affecting different types of development. As part of a repeating cycle, development options are affected directly and indirectly by the judgements and actions of individuals and groups. The indirect path is affected by the degree of physical and cultural separation between the people involved and their ecosystems. The cognitive and operational models that inform their judgements and actions are more likely to be ecocentric where the degree of separation is low, and egocentric (or anthropocentric) where separations are wide.

the emergence of Newtonian science and the so-called Age of Enlightenment, where aspects of nature began to be understood in mathematical and mechanical terms. Early concerns about the schism were voiced by conservationists such as John Muir and Aldo Leopold, who called for a fundamental shift in ethics:

> That land is a community is the basic concept of ecology, but that land is to be loved and respected is an extension of ethics. That land yields a cultural harvest is a fact long known, but latterly often forgotten. (Leopold 1949, viii–ix)

If societies are indeed suffering from the consequences of the human–nature split, then museums ought to be offering societal "therapy" for selfish, altruistic, and pragmatic reasons. On the selfish side, museums rely on the social and ecological systems that have been affected, and anything they can do to make themselves relevant will increase their odds of survival. From an altruistic perspective, museums are ideally positioned to influence the make-up of the systems around them, especially their human and social capital. In pragmatic terms, most museums are obliged to work on behalf of the public good, if only because of their dependence on public funding. The suggestion that museums might play a therapeutic role in society may seem unusual, but in fact is an elaboration of ideas developed by other museum writers (e.g., Silverman 1989, Kaplan, Bardwell & Slakter 1993).

Part of the challenge around sustainability is helping individuals and groups gain an enhanced sense of consciousness about their world, a sense that has been fading for several generations. Museums can help by encouraging people to become more conscious of critical relationships that link them to nature and to other people. Some of the roles that museums can play include being storytellers through non-formal education, providing sanctuaries that inspire reflection, and acting as catalysts to spark needed social change.

THE HUMAN FACTOR EXHIBIT

This section is based on insights that one of us (Sutter) gained through the development of *The Human Factor* exhibit, a series of permanent displays in the new Life Sciences Gallery (LSG) at the Royal Saskatchewan Museum (RSM) in Regina, Saskatchewan. The RSM is a medium-sized museum of natural and human history, and is part of the provincial government. It has an annual visitation of about 150,000, plus some 18,000 students in programs and teacher-supervised visits. Developed to replace a gallery that was damaged by fire in 1990, the new LSG was designed by Blair Fraser Exhibits, Ltd., and opened in 2001. It covers about twelve hundred square metres and consists of an orientation area, a tour of unaltered Saskatchewan landscapes, a section called Global View that looks at how the province is connected to distant locations, and *The Human Factor*, which occupies about 25 per cent of the exhibit space.

The Human Factor is the last part of a gallery storyline about connections and dependencies that keep the Earth and other living systems in a state of dynamic balance (e.g., Lovelock 1987). It is divided into sections called Time Tunnel, Living Planet, Causes of Stress, and Solutions, and includes a computer-based learning centre that is also available on line at www.royalsaskmuseum.ca. The exhibit and learning centre are designed to examine regional and global issues associated with human activity from an ecocentric perspective. They establish prehistoric and historic time frames, describe global processes and imbalances in social and ecological terms, and explore the challenges and potential of sustainable development. The exhibit and the LSG are both described in more detail in Sutter (2000).

The Human Factor exhibit and learning centre appear to be unique on three counts. First, they examine the scope and consequences of human activities by blending ecology, economics, and psychology into a central, coherent message. Second, they identify and assess the industrialized worldview as the root cause of global and regional issues. The exhibit does this through seven sculpted "towers" that reflect and scrutinize industrialized attitudes and actions. Crafted by Dave Gejdos, each tower consists of objects that reflect each theme (Table 1). They are about 2.5 metres tall, including the human figures on top, and are covered with a rough, grey coating for texture and consistency. Finally, the exhibit and the learning centre both stress the importance of restorative economics, individual choices, and our emotional connection to nature.

Considerations that arose during the development of *The Human Factor* fall into four areas. First, to tell this sort of story, the RSM had to take a position around controversial issues such as climate change and the ecological constraints on economic growth. This was easy to justify from a scientific perspective, given the evidence (e.g., Sanderson et al. 2002), but it also introduced an unavoidable bias towards certain facts and set the stage for political or emotional responses. On the political side, senior government officials were informed about possible points of contention, such as the misleading nature of the GDP as a measure of economic health. We were careful not to question the intent of current government policies, and we emphasized that all parts of the story are substantiated by wide bodies of research.

Second, *The Human Factor* had to reflect the central theme of the LSG, which is "dynamic balance through interconnection." To this end, the exhibit focuses on industrialized values, actions, and behaviours that

Tower Title	Imbalances Depicted	Issues Examined
Can we live apart?	PEOPLE vs. nature	Physical and cultural barriers between people and nature.
	INDIVIDUALS vs. communities	Psychological consequences of Individualism
Buy and be happy?	GREED vs. need	Consumerism as fulfilment
	MONEY AS MASTER vs. money as servant	The social power of money
	PRICES vs. reality	Hidden costs
Is bigger better?	GROWTH vs. progress	Expansionism
	GLOBAL vs. local	Global trade
		Power of global corporations and financial markets
Are there no limits?	CONSUMPTION vs. nature as a source	Dwindling supplies
	WASTE vs. nature as a sink	Garbage and pollution
	SLOW & PREDICTABLE vs. rapid & chaotic	The speed of past climate changes
Can science save us?	INFORMATION vs. wisdom	Other "ways of knowing," e.g., slow knowledge
	PRIDE vs. humility	Can we manage ecosystems?
	CONFIDENCE vs. caution	What are acceptable risks? e.g., biotechnology
Ours to conquer?	AGGRESSION, COMPETITION & INDEPENDENCE vs. compassion, cooperation & community	Militarism
		Overlooked skills
	GENDER BIAS vs. gender equality	Poverty and oppression
		Children as security
All for some?	PEOPLE vs. nature	40% of resources appropriated by one species
	HAVES vs. have-nots	Do we have the right?
		Social and economic disparities

Table 1. Topics and imbalances examined by sculpted "towers" in the Causes of Stress section of *The Human Factor* exhibit. For each imbalance, the capitalized term tends to receive more emphasis in Western society.

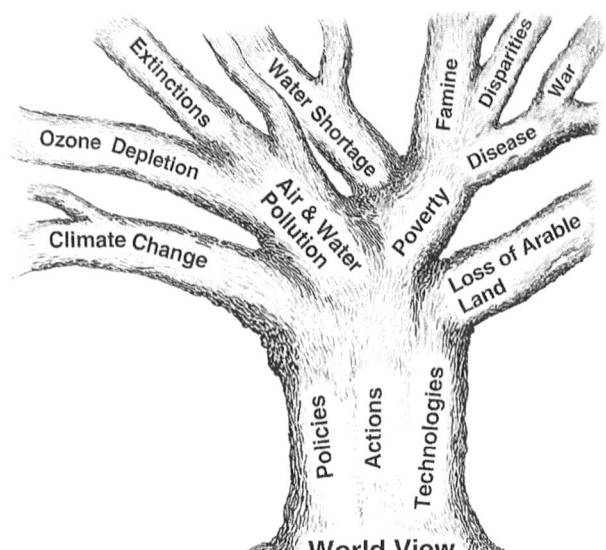

Figure 3. This diagram is on a large wall panel at the start of *The Human Factor* exhibit. It indicates that seemingly disparate problems are actually extensions of policies, actions, and technologies that stem from the industrialized worldview. This assumption is central to the storyline of the exhibit, which includes a detailed assessment of industrialized values, actions, and beliefs (Sutter 2000).

appear to be out of balance, and on the consequences of social and ecological connections that are either frayed or strong. As an example of imbalance, the Can Science Save Us tower (Table 1) suggests that while the objectivity of reductionist science is valuable and necessary to address some problems, societies that rely on it too heavily run the risk of losing "slow" knowledge (Orr 1996) and other valuable "ways of knowing." Other towers focus on frayed connections, including one called Ours To Conquer, which looks at the divisive effects of a social focus on independence, aggression, and competition (Table 1). The benefits of strong connections are evident in the Living Planet area, which looks at processes and relationships that are part of a healthy global ecosystem, and in a Solutions display called Reconnection, which is based on biophilia.[11]

Third, instead of focusing on any one symptom of human activity, such as the loss of biodiversity, we wanted to illustrate how seemingly isolated issues are actually interconnected. The exhibit tells a cause-and-effect story that singles out the industrialized worldview (Winter 1996) as the root cause of a broad range of problems (Fig. 3). The situation is not this clear-cut, since worldviews are also influenced by the problems they produce, but this approach allowed us to tell a comprehensive, integrated story and to elaborate on underlying values and behaviours. It also allowed us to personalize issues that are easily externalized and may have produced a more useful educational tool as a result.

Finally, from an educational perspective, we recognized that emotional responses can have positive and negative repercussions. They can inspire people to reflect on their own values and beliefs, but they can also raise psychological barriers that would hamper the development of new insights (Clinebell 1996). We addressed this by trying to anticipate how visitors might respond, by aiming for a tone of guarded optimism, and by including features designed to heighten and subsequently relieve levels of anxiety (Sutter 2000). The fact that humanity has become a major global force is mentioned at the start of the LSG, partly so visitors are forewarned about the content of *The Human Factor*. To engage visitors and help them feel included, most of the displays in *The Human Factor* are touchable, and interactive, and a central wall panel points out that religious, indigenous, and scientific worldviews often have an ecocentric dimension. At the same time, we stayed away from contentious issues, such as the debate between evolutionists and creationists, and took care to avoid confrontational or antagonistic language. To keep anxiety levels in check, we assumed that images and experiences that speak to the intrinsic value of nature and human goodness would provide a sense of comfort, while details about biophilia, sustainability, success stories, and the importance of daily choices would offer hope.

The LSG is becoming a central part of education programming and evaluation efforts at the RSM. *The Human Factor* section has been challenging from a programming perspective, partly because many of the key points are complex and not easily linked to a tangible object. The notion of an ecological footprint has been helpful in this sense, because staff and visitors can easily relate to it. Evaluation efforts have ranged from using exit surveys, concept maps, and heart-rate recorders to gauge knowledge levels and emotional reactions, to soliciting feedback from grade-school students involved in exhibit development. Early results suggest that visitors may be responding as predicted as they move through the space, that the overall experience is positive, and that some insights may have lasting consequences.

MUSEUMS AND SUSTAINABILITY

Now that we have described what sustainability involves, and how one museum exhibit has tried to address it, we can elaborate on insights and principles that museums might consider as they delve into this area.

First, context is critical. Sustainability issues affect systems that are highly integrated and chaotic,[12] with overlapping physical, biophysical, social, economic, and psycho-spiritual dimensions that cut across social, political, and geographic boundaries. Based on concept maps developed through our Working Group (Appendix A), museum people seem to appreciate the breadth and complexity of the issues, though they may be uncomfortable with the uncertainty and vagueness that goes along with them. Often, the biggest hurdle is getting people to accept that most features of the social and ecological systems they depend on are beyond their control.

The *Human Factor* exhibit includes many examples of interconnection and interdependence. Dominant issues are identified as symptoms of a deeper problem (Fig. 3). Graphs in the Time Tunnel illustrate correlations between global temperature and atmospheric concentrations of carbon dioxide and methane over the last 420,000 years (Petit, et al. 1999). The ecological footprint indicator makes it clear that our global crisis involves more than population growth. A display called Building Blocks and Nested Layers illustrates that life is based on a nested hierarchy that ranges from atoms to the global ecosystem (Rowe 1992). And there are repeated references to emergent properties such as ecosystem health and ecological services (e.g., Costanza, et al. 1997).

Second, when people look sustainability "in the eye," their reactions will reflect attitudes and beliefs that support their worldview, which is unlikely to contribute to sustainability. It follows that efforts to move individuals or groups towards a sustainable path need to bring issues down to a personal level and consider the values and beliefs involved. This is especially important in light of the human–nature split and a general lack of consciousness in highly urbanized societies. Our goal should be to reinforce, embellish, or alter what people know about their world (their ecological literacy) and how they relate to it (their ecological identity), but this needs to be pursued with care and compassion. It is important to be direct about the disastrous nature of some problems, but not to a point that raises emotions or psychological barriers that hamper learning and action. Educators of all types need to consider emotions that might arise, and use approaches that preserve trust and build rapport

This may be part of the reason *The Human Factor* exhibit has been well received. Museums are generally respected and trustworthy institutions, and visitors appear to feel quite comfortable as they take in the nature dioramas that precede *The Human Factor* section. The dioramas seem to provide rich, satisfying experiences, which may be due to biophilia (Wilson 1984), and by the time visitors reach *The Human Factor*, they are often quite open to being challenged about their personal actions and beliefs. Positive visitor responses may also reflect the effort that went into finding common ground between diverse interests, avoiding dogmatic or antagonistic statements, and linking problems and potential solutions to the choices we make as individuals and groups.

Third, as an integral part of complex socio-economic systems, museums ought to be more responsive to their communities. Educators in museums and other settings have assumed that if people are told what the problems are, and are given the skills and information they need to deal with them, they will find common ground between divergent interests and work for a healthier, safer, more humane world. Instead, counter-intuitively, highly educated people are usually part of highly polarized, stress-filled communities. This result is predictable, since complex systems often produce results that are counter-intuitive (Marten 2001). It also suggests that prescriptive approaches to education may be contributing to the problem.

Rather than prescribing solutions – or, worse, passively dispensing information – museums might benefit from encouraging individuals and communities to identify their underlying needs and reflect on the ramifications of their actions. This may be the biggest challenge facing our institutions, because it questions the purpose of museums and flies in the face of momentum that wants to maintain the status quo. It also means playing a less authoritative, and possibly less visible, role in society, as well as basing outcomes and performance measures mostly on community needs and opportunities.

Finally, sustainability has to be measured through robust indicators and adequate feedback mechanisms involving individuals and organizations. These measures are still evolving and present a range of challenges, especially with "cultural" indicators.

There are three spheres within which museums would benefit from reliable indicators. The first relates to the issues, needs and wants of a community at any given point in time. Some of these will be timely in nature – reflecting realities that affect lives, such as an employment crisis, a housing shortage, a rash of domestic violence, high school drop-out rates for certain groups, increasing racism, threatening pollution, funding for public transit, and such. Others will involve more timeless human experiences that shape who we are as individuals and communities. These might include such things as beauty, love, self-esteem, relationships, trust, respect, humility. By conducting a survey of the issues, needs and wants of community, museums can develop public activities to intersect with what is most pressing and relevant for their communities. There are already sets of indicators that help cities monitor their well-being – but museums rarely start their planning from the needs and wants of their communities. Generally, museums are preoccupied with the subject or discipline focus they have set for themselves.

The second sphere of indicators would be designed to assess whether individuals and the larger communities are actually moving towards a "culture of sustainability." For example, measuring pollution levels in air, lakes, and rivers, as well as the prevalence of certain plants and animals in local natural settings, provides insight into the health of the ecosystem. Housing, education, energy usage, food consumption, mortality rates, and other measures reflect the social reality of a population, while income distributions, employment rates, and disposable income provide useful indicators of economic well-being. It is important to remember that these large-scale community indicators become more textured and valuable when they are cross-referenced with major demographic characteristics to determine problems of systemic inequity and dysfunction.

Cultural indicators are still eluding those who are trying to develop indicators of movement towards sustainability. Museums could help to develop such indicators. Some of these might involve assessing individuals'

- awareness of their personal, ethnic, gender, and racial histories;
- propensity for reflecting on environmental, economic, or social-justice issues;
- sense of personal responsibility for the well-being of others, and the community generally;
- understanding and acceptance of significant forces in our lives that are unknowable and uncontrollable (e.g., questions of spirituality).

If museums began to explore these questions, then their public programming could be much more effectively targeted to addressing issues and opportunities that will determine whether our collective future is sustainable or not.

The third sphere of indicators involves understanding how a museum's public program impacts individuals and groups within the community. Part of this is being done by people who are conducting at least one of the three basic forms of audience research in museums – front-end, formative, and summative. Unfortunately, audience research still has a very difficult time being allocated human and financial resources in most museums, and when museums decide to conduct audience research, it is often geared towards marketing and figuring out how best to deliver "cultural commodities" to a target group. This type of market research is not going to move museums towards becoming effective facilitators of culture within communities. Instead, museums need research that helps them understand how to support individuals in cultural reflection and responsible action. Some work has been done in this area (e.g., Worts 1995), but it just scratches the surface. Much remains to be learned about building social capital, or "cultural capital," in our pluralist, urban environments.

CONCLUDING REMARKS

Based on media reports, one might determine that our future is in the hands of scientists, economists, politicians, and business executives –

supported by an army of lawyers. To live sustainably, we will undoubtedly need to make our lives more equitable and efficient, which will require the expertise of such specialists. But even if we solve technical challenges related to production and pollution, we will still be on an unsustainable trajectory. Negotiating a more desirable path will require the conscious participation of individuals seeking to embody the core values of sustainability, especially as ecosystems strive to correct imbalances through famines, floods, epidemics, and other phenomena. The most difficult part of the challenge will involve cultivating worldview(s) in which individuals and groups subscribe to reflective, responsible, and democratic ways of life. This is where museums have a tremendous opportunity to play a vital, new role as cultural facilitator – encouraging individuals to reflect and stimulating communication between people.

Museums could take advantage of the unique position they occupy between the academic world and the general public to help move humanity onto a sustainable path, but not without fundamental changes in their mandates, activities, and organizational structures (see Stapp 1998). Those that continue to operate mainly as object-centred tourist attractions may find it difficult to be involved in sustainability work because of inherent controversies (Worts 1998). At the same time, museums risk becoming marginalized or even irrelevant if they avoid controversy altogether (Weil 2002).

The strategies that museums apply as we move into the twenty-first century are likely to fall somewhere between the traditional focus on exhibitory and collection-building, and more responsive approaches designed to inspire reflection and cultural development. Those that follow traditional lines will be making a tentative commitment that requires no fundamental change in their mandate. They will have to assume that experiences inspired by exhibits and programming are able to restore depleted stocks of human and social capital, such as low levels of ecological literacy, the loss of "slow knowledge," and strained relationships within communities and between people and nature. Their best option might be to highlight historical and contemporary examples of socio-economic and ecological sustainability.

Museums that decide to be more progressive will be closer to the notion of a museum as any setting where the Muses gather to inspire reflection. They will be making a fundamental commitment based on mandates that emphasize personalized, non-formal education, and actions that respond to, and are largely directed by, the needs of their communities. They will be working to rebuild depleted stocks of human and social capital through interactive, community-led activities that identify the common ground between diverse interests, and give rise to appropriate actions and social norms.

APPENDIX A: WORKING GROUP ON MUSEUMS AND SUSTAINABLE COMMUNITIES

Membership

- Thérèse Baribeau and Linda Liboiron, The Biosphère, Environment Canada (Montréal, Québec)
- Anne Breau and Catherine Dumouchel, Canadian Museum of Nature (Ottawa, Ontario)
- Elizabeth Kilvert, Ecological Monitoring and Assessment Network, Environment Canada (Burlington, Ontario)
- Barbara McKean, Royal Botanical Gardens (Burlington, Ontario)
- Diane Pruneau, Université de Moncton (Moncton, New Brunswick)
- Glenn Sutter, Royal Saskatchewan Museum (Regina, Saskatchewan)
- Douglas Worts, Art Gallery of Ontario (Toronto, Ontario)

Activities

Established in 2000, the Working Group on Museums and Sustainable Communities is focusing its efforts on engaging the museum community in Canada in a process of awareness, reflection, learning, sharing of knowledge and experience, capacity-building, and action related to their role in creating a culture of sustainability.

In order to achieve this goal, the working group:

- organizes workshops at the Canadian Museums Association (CMA) Annual Conferences:
    - The Role of Museums in Environmental Education and Sustainability (Ottawa, 2001)
    - Museums and Sustainability – Tools for Action (Calgary, 2002)

- Engaging Your Community in a Culture of Sustainability – Museums as Agents of Change (Winnipeg, 2003)
- has participated in the development of a Framework on Environmental Learning and Sustainability in Canada, and of an Action Plan that was presented, with others from across Canada, at the World Summit on Sustainable Development, Johannesburg, in 2002
- has presented its initiative to the CMA and is being offered the opportunity to have a private website on museums and sustainable communities
- is looking at implementing pilot projects that would provide models on how museums can engage their community in a process leading to a culture of sustainability
- has had discussions with ICOM Canada (which has an ongoing interest in the topic) to look at possible collaborations.

Indicators for Success

- participation in workshops offered by working group, positive feedback from participants and subsequent actions
- visits, repeat visits, and interactions with the Museums and Sustainable Communities website
- implementation of a Museums and Sustainable Communities pilot project
- increased level of awareness and understanding among the museum community in Canada of the concepts of sustainability and sustainable community – and the linkage of these concepts to culture
- number of museums that identify sustainable community as a core part of the Mission Statement
- increasing numbers of initiatives related to this topic in the museum community in Canada
- requests for working group to participate in conferences, training sessions, projects, etc.
- unsolicited inquiries for information
- continued interest and support from the Canadian Museums Association towards this initiative.

ENDNOTES

1 This is how the United Nations defined sustainable development in *Our Common Future: Report of the World Commission on Environment and Development* (1987: 8).
2 For example see: Worts (2003), Leahy (2003), American Association of Museums (2002), Silverman (2002), Sutter (2000), UNESCO (1995).
3 The Working Group on Museums and Sustainable Communities includes professionals and academics from across Canada who have been developing workshops and materials on this topic since 2000. More information is provided in Appendix A.
4 In 1995, with about five billion people on Earth, the average person had an ecological footprint of 2.4 hectares. The available productive land amounted to only 2.0 hectares each, producing a global deficit of 0.4 hectares per person. Now, with a population of more than six billion, we would need 1.3 Earths to sustain the current population with no deficit. If everyone in the world lived like the average Canadian, we would need four whole Earths!
5 The GPI is a revision of the Gross Domestic Product based on factors such as income distribution, the value of household and volunteer work, and the costs of crime and pollution. For details, visit the Redefining Progress website at http://www.rprogress.org/projects/gpi/
6 GDP is the dominant indicator of economic well-being. It is a reliable measure of economic activity, but it says nothing about the impact of that activity on quality of life. The GDP increases, implying economic health, not only when people are employed and buying consumer items, but also when catastrophes like the Exxon Valdez oil-spill occur, when war breaks out, when fires ruin lives, when car accidents lead to more cars being produced, and so on.
7 For the latest information, visit the United Nations Population Information Network website at http://www.un.org/popin/publications.html.
8 "Natural capital" refers to physical resources provided by nature, including freshwater, food, and wildlife. Human capital is a reflection of collective knowledge developed through education, training, and research. Social capital is based on rules, norms, and relationships that affect people and institutions, while manufactured capital refers to buildings, roads, and other parts of the built environment.
9 By development we mean an increase in the quality of economic interactions, as opposed to the physical growth or expansion of an economy.
10 Sheppard (1995) and other psychologists have suggested that the human–nature split has produced a "sick society" that ought to be treated with therapy. They point to signs of a collective "madness" typified by short-sighted actions and beliefs, no appreciation of consequences, always wanting more, selfishness, insecurity, and low self-esteem. Given the complexity of the sustainability challenge, any therapy is bound to include an analysis stage, where issues are broken down to examine their constituent parts.
11 Biophilia – literally, attraction to life – refers to a set of genetically based learning rules that influence our actions and development (Wilson 1984). As an example, people are often more frightened of some animals, such as snakes, even if they have never encountered one, than they are of guns, which are far more dangerous. Biophilia is believed to be a reflection of prehistory, when people lived much closer to nature.

12 Ecosystems, economies, and social systems are characterized by a complex of internal and external connections. Any complex system can exhibit chaotic behaviour, where even slight changes have large and unpredictable consequences.

REFERENCES

American Association of Museums
    2002   *Mastering civic engagement: A challenge to museums*, Washington: AAM.
Clinebell, H.J.
    1996   *Ecotherapy: Healing ourselves, healing the Earth*. Minneapolis: Fortress Press.
Cobb, C., Glickman, M., and Chelog, C.
    2001   *The Genuine Progress Indicator 2000 update*. Redefining Progress Issue Brief.
Costanza, R., Arge, R., de Groot, R., Farber, S., Grasso, M. Hannon, B. et al.
    1997   The value of the world's ecosystem services and natural capital. *Nature, 387*, 253–60.
Daly, Herman
    1999   Steady-state economics. In C. Merchant (Ed.), *Ecology: Key concepts in critical theory* (pp. 86–106). Amherst, N.Y.: Humanity Books.
Holling, C.S.
    1992   Cross-scale morphology, geometry, and dynamics of ecosystems. *Ecological Monographs, 62*, 447–502.
Kaplan, S., Bardwell, L. and Slakter, D.
    1993   The restorative experience as a museum benefit. *Journal of Museum Education, 18*(3), 15–17.
Leahy, S.
    2003   Greening stewardship. *Muse, 21*(1), 22–26.
Leopold, A.
    1949   *A Sand County almanac*. New York: Ballantine Books.
Lovelock, J.E.
    1987   *Gaia: A new look at life on Earth*. New York: Oxford University Press.
Marten, G.G.
    2001   *Human ecology: Basic concepts for sustainable development*. Sterling, VA: Earthscan.
Orr, D.W.
    1996   Slow knowledge. *Conservation Biology, 10*, 699–702.
Petit, J.R., Jouzel, J., Raynaud, D., Barkov, N.I., Barnola, J.-M., Vasile, I. et al.
    1999   Climate and atmospheric history of the past 420,000 years from the Vostok ice core, Antarctica. *Nature, 399*, 429–36.
Rowe, S.
    1992   Biological fallacy: Life = organisms. *BioScience, 42*, 394.
Sanderson, E.W., Jaiteh, M., Levy, M.A., Redford, K.H., Wannebo, A.V., and Woolmer, G.
    2002   The human footprint and the last of the wild. *BioScience, 52*, 891–904.
Sheppard, P.
    1995   Nature and madness. In T. Roszak, M.E. Gomes and A.D. Kanner (Eds.), *Ecopsychology: Restoring the Earth, healing the mind* (pp. 21–40). San Francisco: Sierra Club Books.

Silverman, L.
    1989   Johnny showed us the butterflies: The museum as a family therapy tool. In Barbara H. Butler and Marvin B. Sussman (Eds.), *Museum Visits and Activities* (pp. 131–50). New York: Haworth Press.
    2002   Taking a wider view of museum outcomes and experiences: Theory, research and magic. *JEM*, *23*, 3–8.

Stapp, C.B.
    1998   Museums and community development. *Curator: The Museum Journal*, *41*, 228–34.

Sutter, G.C.
    2000   Ecocentrism, anxiety, and biophilia in environmental education: A museum case-study. In W.L. Filho (Ed.), *Communicating sustainability* (pp. 333–48). New York: Peter Lang.
    2001   Can ecosystem health be ecocentric? *Ecosystem Health*, *7*, 77–78.

United Nations
    1987   *Our common future: Report of the World Commission on Environment and Development*. New York: Oxford University Press.

UNESCO
    1995   *Our creative diversity: Report of the World Commission on Culture and Development*

Wackernagel, M. and Rees, W.
    1995   *Our ecological footprint: Reducing human impact on the Earth*. Gabriola Island: New Society Publishers.

Weil, S.
    2002   Transformed from a cemetery of bric-a-brac. In Stephen Weil, (Ed.) *Making Museums Matter* (pp. 81–90). Washington: Smithsonian Institution Press.

Wilson, E.O.
    1984   *Biophilia: The human bond with other species*. Cambridge: Harvard University Press.

Winter, D.D.
    1996   *Ecological psychology: Healing the split between planet and self*. New York: HaperCollins.

Worts, Douglas
    1995   Extending the frame: Forging a new partnership with the public. In S. Pearce (Ed.), *Art museums* (pp. 164–91). London: Athlone Press.
    1998   On museums, culture and sustainable development. In Lisette Ferera (co-ordinator) *Museums and sustainable communities: Canadian perspectives* (pp. 21–27). Quebec City: ICOM Canada.
    2003   On the brink of irrelevance: Art museum in contemporary society. In L. Tickle, V. Sekules and M. Xanthoudaki (Eds.), *Opening up the cases: Visual arts education in museums and galleries* (pp. 215–31). Dordrecht: Kluwer.

OUT OF SIGHT, OUT OF MIND: HUMAN REMAINS AT THE AUCKLAND MUSEUM – *TE PAPA WHAKAHIKU*

Paul Tapsell

Ahakoa he iti he pounamu
Although small, it is greenstone

This article explores the trajectories of Maori ancestral remains associated with the Auckland War Memorial Museum – Te Papa Whakahiku – since 1869, and the remedies now being applied.

Over the past two hundred or more years *uru-moko (moko mokai)*, *koiwi* and *whakapakoko* (indigenous Maori human remains: cured ancestral heads, crania and post-cranial material, and mummified or desiccated human material) and associated burial *taonga* (carved or woven ancestral items passed down through the generations) were acquired and re-presented in foreign museum-like contexts according to mutually exclusive Western values of ownership, capture, and Otherness. In the early 1980s, the native Other – the majority of whom now lived in metropolitan centres – successfully challenged the "civilized" practice of placing dead on display, finally giving voice to their geographically isolated elders. *Te Maori* was born out of this era, and demonstrated a new way for museums to engage with its audiences, allowing the native voice to enter the exhibition space. Narratives of elders animated aesthetically challenging Maori art to a new level of appreciation, breathing life into the ancestors, thereby transforming Western viewer perceptions at a uniquely human level.

Following in the wake of *Te Maori*, New Zealand's museums began developing vibrant Maori-curated exhibitions which explore codified genealogical narratives – as represented by *taonga* (any tangible or intangible item representing ancestors and estates, maintained by kin elders through the generations) – within a uniquely Maori social-geographic matrix: the *marae* (ceremonial space of encounter between host kin and visitors). Maori ancestral remains that were on display until the early 1980s have since been re-secured in private, customarily maintained museum-storage spaces. In the spirit of partnership, museums have accepted that authority regarding indigenous human remains no longer belongs to museums, but to descendants. Considering how to meaningfully engage with descendants is thus a new challenge for museums. Nurturing and championing socially responsible solutions with indigenous source communities is important. Redressing the morality of holding another culture's ancestors captive is, in fact, a cornerstone of today's shift in Aotearoa New Zealand's museum practice. Whereas Maori communities were "out of sight, out of mind" to metropolitan society, since the Second World War their descendants have now become a significant population in urban New Zealand (Walker 1990). Museums and Maori not only have a shared colonial past – brought into sharp contrast by the Treaty of Waitangi claims process (see I.H. Kawharu 1989 for wider discussions on this topic), but are now seeking new and exciting ways to share the future in order that each may become vital again to forthcoming generations. This article explores that shift by tracing the trajectory of Maori ancestral remains associated with the Auckland War Memorial Museum –Te Papa Whakahiku, from initial collection through to current practice of returning them home and back into the bosom of Papatuanuku (Earth Mother).

Traditionally, Maori secured their remains in *whare koiwi* (mausoleums) or in *ana koiwi* (or *wahi tapu*: secret burial sites) lest they be discovered and utilised for ill purpose by outsiders. In the event of war, kin would attempt to recover their dead in case they fell into enemy hands. To slay an enemy leader in battle and take his head as a trophy – *moko mokai* (cured head of a captured enemy), or create musical instruments from his bones – such as *koauau* (flute), provided the victors with objects of derision. *Moko mokai* in particular, became playthings for children. They were also displayed around cooking areas and in gardens in order to debase the enemy to common food (see Orchiston 1967 for examples).

During peacetime, alliances were sealed not only by *taumau* (political marriage ceremonies) and gifting of *taonga*, but also by repatriation of *moko mokai*. Thereafter, amongst my people of Te Arawa at least, the head completed its transformation to an *uru moko* by being appropriately dressed, mourned over, then laid to rest in *whare koiwi*, alongside heads of other past leaders.

The primary role of *uru moko* and their keeping from one generation to the next was to assist in the amelioration of *marae*-based life-crises at which a strong ancestral presence was required. Two important life-crises were *tangihanga* and *hahunga*. *Tangihanga* was the funeral ritual sometimes lasting upward of five days, whereupon the deceased was then either temporarily buried or taken to a special place until putrefaction was complete. *Hahunga* was the subsequent public display of the scraped and painted remains, prior to final concealment in *ana koiwi*. During these crises, *uru moko* were retrieved, dressed in finest cloaks to appear life-like, and took up guard over the *tupapaku* (body lying in state) or *koiwi* while resting on the *marae*.

Taonga associated with great leaders played an important role in maintaining the well-being of the kin group. They often accompanied the remains of their wearers into death, sometimes for generations, until they too reappeared during relevant life-crisis rituals (Tapsell 1997). During *tangihanga* in particular, *taonga* assisted elders in the ceremonial "collapsing" of the *marae* space, allowing descendants to ritually engage with more distant ancestors than those represented by *uru moko*. *Taonga* thus reinforced a tribe's wider, common genealogical relationship with other groups, with their *whenua* (ancestral sea/landscape) and, on certain occasions, with *manuhiri* (honoured visitors). They ensured ancestors were present to embrace the *wairua* (spirit; soul) of the recently departed, so he or she could be guided safely back to Hawaiki, the spiritual homeland (ibid.).

In the early European contact years (1790–1830s), major depopulation occurred as a result of introduced diseases and firearms. Unprecedented crises arose, to which Maori had no immediate answer. The arrival of missionaries provided new pathways of amelioration that eventually led to the recovery of communities and consequent synthesis of Christianity into the Maori spiritual belief system (Tapsell 2002). *Whare koiwi* and *ana koiwi* were replaced by *urupa* (publicly accessible cemeteries), *hahunga* superseded by *tohu kohatu* (Christianised unveilings of headstones on graves), and ancestral portraits and photographs supplanted *uru moko*. *Marae*, on the other hand, continued as a political and spiritual focus of the community without cultural disruption.

By the mid-1850s, Maori across Aotearoa had generally adopted Christian burial practices and the ancestral remains not gathered up and reburied in cemeteries were left to rest in their hidden sanctuaries as a mark of respect to a former realm of beliefs. Although modified, *tangihanga* remains to this day the ritual foundation of *marae*. Despite colonisation, *taonga* continue to bind living with the dead, bridge the past with the present and ceremonially reinforce tribal identity as represented by *marae*, to surrounding ancestral lands, waterways and resources (Tapsell 1998).

Half a world away in England, exotic human remains collected by scientists on South Pacific voyages of exploration and even, it seems, on early missionary journeys, went on display in museums (Orchiston 1967; Auckland Museum Archives MA 95/43/3 Av.2.6.25). Later whalers, sealers, and traders increased the volume of Maori human remains taken to Europe (Orchiston 1967, Robley 1896). The pre-1840 dark years of Maori inter-tribal musket warfare provided opportunity for kin adversaries not only to settle old scores, but also to debase the heads of their enemies as trade items with foreigners. The better they were tattooed, the greater the price they fetched – measured in muskets, powder, and shot – thus improving opportunity to capitalize on one's enemies even further. The fear that gripped kin communities during these times must have been horrific. Tribal leaders carried the finest *moko* (facial tattoo) and were consequently ever looking over their shoulders, lest one of their own might be tempted. Even those with clear faces were vulnerable, because if captured, they were sometimes tattooed and then killed anyway (Robley 1896). By 1830, hundreds of *moko mokai* had been internationally traded via Sydney, Australia, finding their way into major European and North American private collections and museums. Interestingly, the overseas exhibiting of *moko mokai* to titillate the curious not only boosted museums' popularity, fuelling a growing market for more, but also mirrored

Maori customary practice of displaying captured heads as trophies of war – items of profanity – upon whom all and sundry could gaze.

By 1831, supply of *moko mokai* had generally dwindled now that most tribes had become equipped with firearms, restoring the balance of power. The 1820s crisis of possible annihilation was either countered or the kin group had ceased to exist. The surviving tribes of Aotearoa synthesized Christianity within their wider, genealogically ordered value system, shifting Maori toward more peaceful modes of trade and opportunity. Nevertheless, demand for *moko mokai* remained, and traders like Joe Rowe went to great lengths to try to procure heads, ultimately losing his own in the process (Robley 1896: 178–79). Warfare was still raging in the Bay of Plenty, out of which another trader, Captain Jack, purchased a sack of heads that belonged to fallen kin visiting from Ngapuhi (ibid.: 179). The resulting public commotion, both in the Bay of Islands and then in Sydney, resulted in the Governor of New South Wales issuing a proclamation banning any further trade of Maori heads out of New Zealand. He also called for all heads already in Sydney to be immediately returned to the schooner *Prince of Denmark*, in order they might be restored to their relations (ibid.). Aside from purchases made by Commodore Wilkes of the United States in 1839, and perhaps other chance acquisitions reported to have occurred as late as the 1870s (Barrow 1964: 44), all further trade of *moko mokai* had ceased by the time the Treaty of Waitangi had been signed in 1840, declaring New Zealand a sovereign colony of the British Crown.

In the early nineteenth century, the rise of scientific interest in typologizing mankind required the acquisition of large, representative collections of remains from around the world. This interest, coupled with the market provided by phrenologists, fuelled the collecting of Maori remains and their donation to institutions in Europe. In the later nineteenth century this collecting accelerated, with the introduction of Darwinian theories of evolution and the belief that even greater sample size was required to isolate racial characteristics that, despite continued and ever more intricate systems of measurement, were becoming more and more illusory (Fforde n.d.). Collecting remains was a particular desideratum for scientific voyages at the time. Leading scientists at institutions such as the Royal College of Surgeons, the University of Edinburgh, the University of Oxford, the University of Cambridge, and the British

Museum (Natural History) sought to demonstrate evolutionary sequences through the measurement and often display of crania (Fforde 1997).

In New Zealand from the 1870s onward, museum-associated professionals like Julius von Haast (Canterbury), James Hector (Wellington) and Thomas Cheeseman (Auckland) enthusiastically responded to an increasing European market for Maori human remains. They did this by leading or commissioning local expeditions to locate *ana koiwi*, retrieving their contents, and using them as currency to augment the European sections of their own museums. Not surprisingly, the Auckland Museum (established in 1852) – being the oldest in New Zealand, situated in the most densely Maori-populated region of the country, overlooking the nation's largest seaport – played a pivotal role in the establishment of international trade of Maori human remains and *taonga* to overseas institutions. In the late 1870s, Auckland Museum's new curator, Cheeseman, embarked on a strategy to build up his institution's exotic collections. As described in the Annual Report for 1877–78 (p. 10):

> Arrangements have been made by the curator for interchanges with most of the principal European museums, and a considerable number of specimens in all branches of natural history have been specially collected for this purpose.

Maori crania were one of the items offered to overseas museums, and were greatly in demand. Three examples serve to illustrate this trade:

> My Dear Sir, ... During the approaching spring and summer months I hope to visit many of the old burial caves of the Maoris to the north of Auckland, and will send you a more extensive collection and also a number of the[ir] weapons and tools.... The case of the prehistoric skulls, and those of the Polynesians collected by the expedition of Durmont D'Urville would be very valuable to us. But as our Museum has only lately been established, almost anything bearing upon anthropology would be gladly received. (Letter extract: Cheeseman to De Quatrefages, Paris Natural History Museum, 23 July 1877)

> Dear Sir, On the part of the Auckland Museum, I take the liberty of writing to you to ascertain whether it would be possible to open an

exchange of specimens with the museum under your charge ... I could send: Pros thermadera and other genera ... 2nd New Zealand insects ... 3rd New Zealand shells ... 4th Ethnological specimens relating to the Maori race – also a series of their crania etc.... We principally wish to have in return specimens of South European mammals and birds, but we should gladly receive specimens in all branches of Natural History. (Letter extract: Cheeseman to Giglioli, Florence Museum, 19 September 1877)

Dear Sir, I safely received your letter of December 14th relative to the exchange of specimens. As I gathered from it that your chief desideratum was a series of Maori Crania I at once set about collecting a number, and now have the pleasure of informing you that I have shipped a case containing 21 good skulls to our agent at San Francisco.... Should you require more Crania I can easily obtain them. (Letter extract: Cheeseman to Prof. Joseph Henry, Smithsonian, 30 April 1878)

As a result of such letters, the Auckland Museum solicited all manner of antiquities, scientific specimens (including exotic indigenous remains, botanical and zoological samples) and museological curiosities from around the world in exchange for items particular to New Zealand, not least crania and accompanying *taonga* removed from *ana koiwi* without appropriate Maori authority. Cheeseman, being the meticulous scientist he was, nevertheless ensured that the exported remains were accompanied by specific provenance details, in one instance even naming the burial cave from where *koiwi* were obtained.

It appears that the reason Cheeseman could provide such large quantities of crania and associated burial items was because he had a network of agents working on the ground acting on his behalf. In particular, two characters, James Curruth and C. Tothill, assisted Cheeseman in the clandestine collection and shipping of crania to Auckland for international trade:

It is probable, I think, that a few more skulls may yet be got ... I have not seen any of the gum diggers myself, but have sent a message to one, stating that if the skulls are brought to me I shall pay for them –

160 OUT OF SIGHT, OUT OF MIND

> I may mention that the gum diggers are very shy about the matter as they have a good deal of intercourse with the Maoris. Indeed it would not do at all for them to take the skulls to the settlement, and pack them for Auckland. (Letter extract: James Curruth to Cheeseman, 4 June 1878)

> Dear Sir, I received your letter … and the box of skulls had turned up a few days previously. What I have got altogether will satisfy the orders that I have and leave a balance over, but it is just possible that there may be more demands … (Letter extract: Cheeseman to C. Tothill Esq., 4 May 1885)

Upon receipt of remains and *taonga*, Cheeseman accessioned what the Auckland Museum required, then stockpiled the rest for scientific trade with famous institutions around the world:

> My Dear Sir, Several months ago I received a letter from you inquiring whether a series of Maori crania could be obtained for the British Museum … I have at least succeeded in obtaining a very good series indeed of 30 crania…. The crania are from a Maori burial cave called…. This cave is only a few miles distant from the one from which I obtained the skulls sent to the College of Surgeons. I have known of it for sometime, but until lately some Maoris resided in the immediate vicinity, and kept such good watch that it would not have been prudent to have made an attempt to secure the skulls … (Letter extract: Cheeseman to Prof. Flower FRS, 25 May 1885)

Given also the market demand for crania and associated *taonga*, it is not unlikely that Cheeseman's agents kept back some of the best material recovered during such expeditions. International dealers like Eric Craig, who in particular had set up his own "Curiosity Shop" directly beside the Auckland Museum (Princes Street) in the late 1880s, offered all manner of things for sale, including "Maori Skulls."

Independently collected items that passed through dealers such as Craig eventually found their way into European and North American private collections and auction houses. It is interesting that until the 1980s, the commercial value of internationally traded *taonga* took no account of the inherent genealogical values that often remained attached to each item. From time to time, international trajectories of human remains and *taonga* circulating in museums or through auction houses have crossed paths with descendants, creating brief but poignant reunions. As a result of *Te Maori*, however, overseas audiences began to appreciate the importance of this genealogical dimension and possible associations of *taonga* with famous ancestors. Meanwhile, Maori human remains displayed in museums have quietly disappeared from sight for fear of adverse protest, as new generations of Maori demonstrated far less patience than their predecessors (Tapsell 1998). Most museums in Aotearoa New Zealand, nonetheless, took heart from the *Te Maori* experience, and the more adventurous explored new ways of displaying *taonga* in conjunction with descendants, better reflecting the values of the context from which they arose. Involving source Maori communities unleashed new opportunities for museums to pursue. But the unexpected consequence – from a Maori perspective, at least – was the escalation in commercial value of any *taonga* still carrying genealogically layered narratives. This increase inhibited, rather than facilitated, any potential for purchase-return to source community control.

As stated in the above correspondence, the late-nineteenth-century raiding of *ana koiwi* by museum-motivated collectors did not go unnoticed. Maori attempted to overcome such desecrations by mounting guard, relocating their dead to more remote caves, sealing the entranceways, or re-burying them in *urupa* close to their *marae*. But times continued to be turbulent in light of the 1860s wars against the Crown/New Zealand Government (Belich 1986) and then the introduction of the Native Land Court system that further ruptured community cohesion (I.H. Kawharu 1977). It appears that some collectors took advantage of Maori community upheaval and disintegration by offering aggrieved kin pecuniary benefit in exchange not only for *taonga*, but in some cases assistance with locating *ana koiwi* and removing their contents:

> Two Maoris, who had become sufficiently Europeanised to be willing to renounce their national and religious principles for gold, led me one night to a cave.... There I found four mummies [*whakapakoko*], of which two were in a state of perfect preservation. The undertaking was a dangerous one, for discovery might have cost me my life. In

> the night I had the mummies removed from the spot and then well hidden; during the next night they were carried still farther away, and so on, until they had been brought safely over the boundaries of Maoriland. But even then I kept them cautiously hidden from sight right up to the time of my departure from New Zealand. (Reischek (April 1882), in King 1981: 96–97)

Generally, colonial museums in the nineteenth century were not seen as attractive places to send human remains and *taonga*, mainly because they were considered neither prestigious nor socially influential (Fforde 1997). Consequently, collectors like Reischek sought to make a name for themselves in their European homelands by offering their collections to nationally recognised institutions in return for scientific kudos and society benefits. By donating to European institutions, amateur scientists in the colonies also received benefits in the form of prestigious contact with leading scholars, as well as more material benefits such as journal publications.

Up until Cheeseman's death in 1924, it appears that the Auckland Museum's accessioning of human remains was low (145 in forty years) compared to its later acquisition history. From the 1920s onwards, collecting by European institutions had dramatically decreased (Fforde n.d.). Measurement of skeletal remains as a method of isolating racial characteristics, examining human evolution and understanding human difference, was becoming increasingly problematic amongst scientists of the day. Even the existence of "race" was being questioned (Stocking 1968, 1988). However, the failure of the market, and the rising status of museums in the colonies, meant that local collections began to substantially rise, not least in New Zealand. From the late 1920s onward, there was a dramatic increase in human remains accessioned by the Auckland Museum (for example, approximately fifty-five in 1928 alone). Given New Zealand's growing sense of national identity – forged out of the First World War, resulting not least in the construction of the Auckland War Memorial Museum (1929) to replace the old Princes Street premises – collectors and public alike keenly supported their new museum by donating all manner of things, not least human remains. Also to emerge around this time was a new academic elite. The museum and its institute became a primary benefactor of their field research and scholarship.

During this collecting resurgence, the science of archaeology arose, providing a new rationale to investigate Maori burial sites. A new generation of Maori now found themselves in conflict with values being championed by museums. In one instance, a community took its protest to government and solicited assistance from influential Maori leader, Sir Apirana Ngata. As a result, Ngata petitioned the Auckland Museum to intervene, and even wrote directly to the offender asking him to desist:

> Dear Sir, Complaints have reached me from the Natives that you are desecrating a graveyard.... The Natives claim that their dead have been desecrated and the officer, who says the place is riddled with excavations, located human bones that have evidently been unearthed. I should be glad if you would at once desist from offending the susceptibilities of the Natives and cease from excavation on the ground in question. (Letter extract forwarded to Archey, Auckland Museum: A.T. Ngata (Native Minister of New Zealand House of Representatives) to Mr S.M. Hovell, Esq., Waihi 14 December 1932)

It appears, however, that Ngata's efforts had little impact. Wider correspondence of the time indicates that one of the museum's influential benefactors, George Graham, actually encouraged tribes to cooperate and allow their burial-associated *taonga* to be placed in the museum. There was otherwise risk, Graham argued, that everything could be lost to less scrupulous collectors:

> Greetings: Your letter to hand has been read and considered. Listen hereto: As to your complaints about transgressions on your people's urupas – you are correct in part. But be reasonable. How can the pakeha [European] tell what is tapu [restricted], what is noa [free of restriction or sanctions] – & what is urupa, & what is not. Those things of value there should be collected by you and yours otherwise the proverb applies.... "Treasured plumes of Mahina washed up like driftwood will not be returned" ... As the pakeha is a meddlesome, inquisitive person, he respects not ancient dead remains & belongings of former people found in long disused urupas & kaingas [villages]. So therefore your people should not delay, but collect all those remains of the dead & gather them into your common

urupa.... Your [ancient burial sites] must be no longer secure – new times bring new manners, & the rigidity of tapu is now non-existent, nor possible to perpetuate. If you therefore value your ... heirlooms [*taonga*] – be they weapons, or ornaments, or garments or what not – they will surely perish if not securely preserved in this "place of things gathered" [.e. the Auckland Museum]. (Letter extract: Geo Graham (Secretary of the Pakeha organization called Te Akarana Maori Association) to leader of Nga Uri-a-Hau of Ngati Whatua, Kaipara, 21 December 1932)

Not surprisingly, the Kaipara leader never replied to the invitation to bring his peoples' *taonga* to the Auckland Museum, nor, to the dismay of Graham, did he reveal the site of the most revered *ana koiwi* in the Kaipara. Notwithstanding continuous but muted protests by kin communities throughout Aotearoa New Zealand, archaeologists continued exploring, locating and removing material from burial grounds (*wahi tapu*) for many more decades. Not until the late 1980s – in the wake of Maori protests (Walker 1990), *Te Maori* Exhibition (Tapsell 1995) and a Maori-sympathetic Labour Government (1984–87) – did museum-university sponsored burial site investigation and removal of *koiwi* and associated *taonga* come to an end.

While the Auckland Museum was busy engaging with the rest of the world, the local Maori community, Ngati Whatua O Orakei, were enduring their own struggle as a result of colonization and urban Auckland development. The measure of any Maori communities' *mana* (customary authority) is in its generosity of giving, or what Maori call *manaakitanga*. In 1951, Ngati Whatua O Orakei were evicted from their *papakainga* (village) and *marae*:

The necessary proclamations were issued in March, all appeals had been heard and summarily dismissed by May, and the meeting house was burnt down in December. At the time, the wells of anguish in the hearts of those who gathered mutely above the cinders of their meeting house seemed likely to never run dry. And perhaps those who came to pass judgment on the ensuing apathy of these people need not have looked further for causes. (I.H. Kawharu 1975: 12)

Surrounding ancestral lands were converted into coastline suburbs for the wealthy, and the unearthed ancestral remains collected in cardboard boxes and stored at the University of Auckland. In less than a hundred years, Ngati Whatua's tenure over tens of thousands of acres was reduced, by 1951, to a quarter acre cemetery in Okahu Bay. Bush made way for farmland, which in turn made way for quarries, roads, and urban development. Meanwhile, lakes, harbours, wetlands, and estuaries were converted to Crown title without any legal recourse. Furthermore, by this time dozens of formerly secret *ana koiwi* and burial sites had been disturbed. Ancestral remains of major tribal groups like Horouta, Kurahaupo, Te Arawa, Tainui, Mataatua, Aotea, and Ngati Whatua, representing thirty generations of sequential isthmus occupation, were unearthed. Whereas the law required police to investigate such scenes to confirm whether the *koiwi* (crania and post-crania) were pre-European contact, there was no requirement for Ngati Whatua O Orakei to be contacted to provide spiritual service and facilitate appropriate reburial, even though it was their customary duty as *tangata whenua* (local people). Instead, when police had finished their work, *koiwi* were generally passed without ceremony over to either the Auckland Museum or the University of Auckland's Archaeology Department (eventually also ending up in the museum) in the belief they were only of scientific value.

In 1991, the Crown acknowledged the findings of the Waitangi Tribunal and returned land to the Orakei community, along with an offer of three million dollars compensation. Most importantly, title to Ngati Whatua's *marae* was returned (Orakei Act 1991). With their *marae* restored, a new generation of Orakei descendants began making proper use of the *marae*, now that they were able to apply *manaakitanga* appropriately. Thereafter, Orakei's three foundations of customary identity were re-established: the *marae*, *manaaki*, and *urupa*. After a hundred years, Ngati Whatua O Orakei was finally back in a position to meaningfully take responsibility again for all things of importance to Maori occurring in Auckland.

Institutions like the Auckland Museum have come to recognize such customary rights and responsibilities. When an Orakei representative learnt that the museum was reviewing its legislation, an opportunity arose to petition the museum for change in the way Maori values were to be represented in the institution's governance. New legislation was eventually passed in 1996, and of the new, ten-member Trust Board, one was to be a Maori representative. It was deemed that the Taumata-a-Iwi – the museum's own Maori advisory committee as defined in the Auckland War Memorial Act 1996 – was responsible for that appointment. This did not occur, however, until 1997, after the Taumata-a-Iwi was officially constituted. Three representatives are nominated by Ngati Whatua O Orakei, and by their invitation, there is one representative each from neighbouring tribes Tainui and Ngati Paoa (M. Kawharu 2002). The Maori representative to the Auckland Museum Trust Board is appointed by the Taumata-a-Iwi.

Under its 1996 legislation, the Auckland Museum Trust Board is statutorily required to seek advice and take due regard from its Taumata-a-Iwi on any issues concerning Maori. In 2001, the Auckland Museum Trust Board became cognizant of its responsibilities to Maori, and developed its own Guiding Principles for the Trust Board's Relationship with its legislated Maori advisors (Auckland War Museum Annual Plan 2002/2003). At the same time, the Taumata-a-Iwi revised its 1998 *Kaupapa*, to complement the Trust Board initiative. From this platform of aligned principles, Maori-related governance policies concerning all aspects of the museum were drafted, ratified by the Taumata-a-Iwi, confirmed by the Trust Board, and integrated into existing policies in mid 2002. Thereafter, related Maori operational policies and procedures – born out of five years of Taumata-a-Iwi and wider Maori community interactions – were integrated throughout the organization. This ensures that all employees who carry out any operation in the museum involving Maori values have a policy framework to which they can refer and by which they can proceed accordingly. These integrated principles and policies now provide a robust vehicle by which the museum and its Taumata-a-Iwi responsibly protect Maori values, not least the appropriate return home of all associated ancestral remains.

Proactive engagement by the Auckland Museum with Maori is a primary goal of the Taumata-a-Iwi. Since the 1980s, the museum has found itself time and again caught in reactive situations, often responding in a manner that provided neither party with sustainable solutions, nor the opportunity to develop goodwill. With the formation of the Taumata-a-Iwi, the museum finally provided itself with a mechanism by which to begin engaging with the Maori community in a more positive manner. However, until the continuing custody of *koiwi* is redressed, sustainable engagement with Maori will remain illusive. So long as museums continue to hold their ancestors, Maori communities will remain uncomfortable developing relationships with museums like Auckland, lest they be perceived to be aiding and abetting the status quo of ancestral capture.

The question before the Auckland Museum today is how to begin redressing one-hundred-plus years of inappropriate collecting of remains and associated *taonga*. A human-remains policy has been developed to take account of descendant communities' expectations. It has built upon actual returns, such as the return of *koiwi* to Ngati Naho-Tainui in 2001 (AWMM Repatriation File 2001). Central to the policy is direct consultation between the museum and community elders in order to build relationships of trust that uphold Maori values surrounding the dead. In its first demonstration of intent, all of the ancestral remains within the museum were ceremonially shifted from Ethnology Store, in the rear of the building, to a newly consecrated space at the front, named Te Urupa. With this 2001 relocation, the ancestral remains moved one step closer to returning home.

Re-centralization has enabled the museum to begin the arduous task of assembling a comprehensive inventory of all archival documentation associated with the hundreds of Maori human remains collected since 1869. In 2002, the Auckland Museum's Human Remains Database Project (Stage 1) began. The first major challenge met was rejoining ancestors with archival records so that, for the first time, an accurate picture is now available of not only how, but from where *koiwi* associated with the museum were collected. Under the direction of the Taumata-a-Iwi, the contracted researcher, Cressida Fforde, has geographically reordered all the remains in preparation for return. A comprehensive electronic file has also been assembled, complete with correspondence, field notes, and inventory records, outlining details of every ancestral remain, Maori and other, currently resting in Te Urupa. The database reveals that in over 90 per cent of cases the exact location from where the *koiwi* originated is documented. International correspondence was also uncovered concerning hundreds of *koiwi* Auckland Museum traded elsewhere in return for exotic collections (Fforde 2003).

On 17 February 2003, Stage I of the database project was completed and presented to the Taumata-a-Iwi at a special *hui* (Maori ceremonial gathering) on Orakei Marae. The project accounted for all indigenous remains currently resting in the museum. At the *hui*, the Taumata-a-Iwi noted that the *wairua* once associated with *koiwi* as living beings have, in most cases, been returned (*tangihanga* and *hahunga*) to Hawaiki by their kin. The Taumata-a-Iwi concluded that their primary duty is to facilitate return of ancestral remains to communities in order that the physical reintegration of *koiwi* (human bone) with Papatuanuku (Earth Mother) can be completed. In some cases, communities may decide that another *tangihanga* is necessary. It is anticipated, however, that in the majority of cases, elders will request their *koiwi* to be discreetly taken directly to the community's *urupa*. There they will be ceremonially received and laid to rest.

From July 2003, accurate data-basing of all known Maori human remains traded by the Auckland Museum to other parts of the world (Stage II) is scheduled to commence. It is hoped that overseas institutions will eventually accept that withholding such ancestral human remains, collected against the wishes of descendants, is scientifically and morally unjustifiable. The research will ensure that the Auckland Museum and its Taumata-a-Iwi will be ready to facilitate proactive engagement when the time arises.

The Taumata-a-Iwi has initiated an accountable management process by which the museum can return all remains to source. The museum's commitment and pathway forward are clear, but it will take years, and many resources, to see it through to completion. Fortunately, from the Trust Board level through to volunteers, there is a growing understanding and appreciation of integrated Maori values, starting with the returning home of the dead. Policies could not work without relevant commitment. By the time the new Grand Atrium opens in 2006, the majority of the *koiwi* will have begun their travels home.

This article has traced the trajectory of Maori ancestral remains associated with the Auckland War Memorial Museum – Te Papa Whakahiku, from initial collection through to today. It has also raised a concern. It appears that museums now accept that responsibility for human remains lies with descendant communities, but what about the *taonga* that once accompanied them? These *taonga* represented the very essence of kin identity to surrounding ancestral landscapes reaching back in some instances thirty or more generations. Whereas *koiwi* were expected to reintegrate with the earth, *taonga* travelled through the generations gathering greater value over time. In pre-contact times, the safest place to keep them was with the dead, where they were spiritually protected – *tapu* – until such time as they were again needed by the living. *Ana koiwi* were filled with *taonga*, especially greenstone pendants like *hei tiki*, other neck ornaments, eardrops, and weapons like *mere*. They were rare and treasured. Seldom were they ever lost. In such cases, narratives of loss were passed down through the generations. *Pounamu* (greenstone) items, in particular, were primary portals to ancestral identity, and played a key role in ameliorating life-crises, be it war, marriage, or death. Under the strict control of appropriately trained elders, called *tohunga*, they would appear for a time and then just as quickly disappear, sometimes for generations. During New Zealand's pre-Second World War years of colonization, many *ana koiwi* throughout Aotearoa New Zealand were disturbed, and their contents emptied. The thousands of Maori ancestral remains scattered throughout the world's museums are evidence of this fact. But seldom is there mention of the *taonga* that would have once rested beside them. Tribes are now generally destitute of such things. Where are they today? Are they in museums, accessioned without mention of the burial places from where they came? Or did collectors, fossickers, farmers, or developers hold onto them while releasing the less socially acceptable *koiwi* to science? And from where did all the greenstone items still circulating overseas, or in private collections, originate? More questions than answers, but there are moves in the right direction.

> *Ka piti hono, tatai hono*
> *Te hunga mate ki te hunga wairua*
> *Ka piti hono, tatai hono*
> *Tatou te hunga ora ki a tatou.*

> Join together, bind together
> The dead with the dead
> Join together, bind together
> The living with all things living.

GLOSSARY

ana koiwi	concealed burial sites, usually caves
hahunga	ritual preparation and display of scraped and painted remains
Hawaiki	spiritual homeland of the Maori
kaitiakitanga	customary guardianship over resources and *taonga*
koauau	small flute generally made from bone
koiwi	bones: crania and post-cranial material
mana	prestige, ancestral authority of a tribe
manaaki(tanga)	care for, look after visitors (host responsibilities)
manuhiri	honoured non-kin visitors
marae	ceremonial space of encounter between host kin and visitors, ritually maintained and negotiated by home elders
mere	greenstone striking weapon once used by fighting leaders
mihimihi	ritual speeches of male elders on *marae*
moko	facial tattoo formerly signifying rank
moko mokai	cured head of a captured male enemy
Ngati Whatua O Orakei	The people of Whatua at Orakei consisting of three related hapu (kin groups): Te Taou, Nga Oho and Te Uringutu
noa	free of ancestral presence, restriction or sanctions
Pakeha	New Zealander of European descent
papakainga	home village
Papatuanuku	Papa, Earth Mother
Tamaki	Maori name for Auckland
tangata whenua	people of the land, local kin
tangihanga	death-mourning ritual on a *marae* lasting several days
taonga	any tangible or intangible item representing ancestors and estates maintained by kin elders through the generations

tapu	protect, respect, set apart, restricted, ancestral presence
Tainui	tribal confederation of Waikato region
Taumata-a-Iwi	Auckland Museum's Maori Advisory Committee
taumau	arranged marriage between two tribes
Te Arawa	tribal confederation of the Bay of Plenty/Rotorua region
Te Maori	exhibition of *taonga* that toured U.S.A. and N.Z., 1984–87
Te Papa Whakahiku	Maori name of Auckland War Memorial Museum
Te Urupa	Auckland Museum's consecrated space for ancestral remains
tohu kohatu	Christianized unveilings of headstones on graves
tohunga	spiritual leader, controls *tapu* and supports kin leadership
tupapaku	body laying in state at *tangihanga*
uru-moko	cured head of a revered male ancestor
urupa	Maori cemeteries
wahi tapu	site usually associated with burial, battle or special occasion
wairua	spirit; soul
whakapakoko	mummified or desiccated human material
whare koiwi	carved mausoleums beside the *marae*
whenua	land, afterbirth, placenta of Papatuanuku; Ancestral sea/landscape and associated resources

REFERENCES

Annual Report of the Auckland Institute and Museum. 1877–78.
    1878   Auckland.
Auckland War Memorial Act 1996, No. 4 – Local. Wellington. New Zealand Government.
    2 September 1996.
Auckland War Memorial Museum Annual Plan 2003/2004. Auckland: David Bateman.
Barrow, T.
    1964.   *The decorative arts of the New Zealand Maori.* Wellington: Reed.

Belich, J.
    1986   *The New Zealand Wars*. Auckland: Auckland University Press.
Cleaves' Auckland Directory 1890. Auckland: Cleaves.
Fforde, C.
    1997   *Controlling the dead: An analysis of the collections and repatriation of Aboriginal human remains*. Ph.D. thesis, University of Southampton.
    2003   *The Auckland War Memorial Museum – Te Papa Whakahiku Collection of Human Remains*. Consultation Report. 12 March 2003.
    n.d.   *Controlling the dead: Archaeology and the reburial issue*. Manuscript in preparation for publication.
Flower, W.H.
    1885   Classification of the varieties of the human species. President's Address. *Journal of the Anthropological Institute*, 14, 378–94.
Gudgeon, T.W
    1885   *The history and the doings of the Maoris*. Auckland.
Kawharu, I.H.
    1975   *Orakei: A Ngati Whatua community*. Wellington: New Zealand Council for Educational Research.
    1977   *Maori land tenure*. Oxford: Clarendon Press.
    1989   *Waitangi: Maori and Pakeha perspectives of the Treaty of Waitangi*. I.H. Kawharu (Ed.). Auckland: Oxford: University Press.
Kawharu, M.
    2002   Indigenous governance in museums: a case study, the Auckland War Memorial Museum. In C. Fforde, J. Herbert and P. Turnbull (Eds.), *The Dead and their Possessions: Repatriation in principle, policy and practice* (pp. 293–302). London: Routledge.
King, M.
    1981   *The Collector: A biography of Andreas Reischek*. Auckland: Hodder & Stoughton.
Metro. (monthly magazine) N. Legat (Ed.). Auckland: ACP Media.
New Zealand Herald. (daily newspaper) G. Ellis (Ed.). Auckland: Wilson & Horton.
Orakei Act 1991. Wellington: New Zealand Government.
Orchiston, D.W.
    1967   Preserved human heads of the New Zealand Maori. *Journal of the Polynesian Society*. 76, 297–329.
Robley, H.G.
    1896   *Moko; or Maori tattooing*. London: Chapman and Hall.
Stocking, G.W.
    1968   *Race, culture and evolution*. Chicago: University of Chicago Press.
    1988   Bones, bodies and behaviour. In G.W. Stocking (Ed.), *Bones, bodies and behaviour* (pp. 3–17). Madison: Wisconsin University Press.
Tapsell, P.
    1995   *Pukaki: Ko te Taonga o Ngati Whakaue*. M.A. thesis. University of Auckland.
    1997   The Flight of Pareraututu. *Journal of the Polynesian Society*, 106(4), 223–374.
    1998   *Taonga: A tribal response to museums*. Unpublished D.Phil Dissertation. University of Oxford.
    2002   Marae and tribal identity in urban Aotearoa/New Zealand. In *Moral Communities*. Special Issue of *Pacific* Studies. J. Mordell (Ed.), 25(1/2) – March/June 2002. Hawaii. Brigham Young University, 141–71.

Taylor. R.
    1855   *Te Ika a Maui*. London. Wertheim and MacIntosh.

Turner, W.
    1886   *Comparative osteology of races of men (comprising parts XXIX and XLVII of the zoological series of reports on the scientific results of the voyage of HMS Challenger)*. Edinburgh.

Walker, R.J.
    1990   *Ka Whawhai Tonu Matou: Struggle without end*. Auckland: Penguin.

Wilkes, C.
    1850   *Narrative of the United States exploring expedition*. Vol. II. Philadelphia: Sea and Blanchard.

AUCKLAND MUSEUM ARCHIVES

B/2028, B/2029 in Collectors: Craig – Ethnology
MA 95/43/3 Av.2.6.25
MA 95/43/6 AV.2.6.107
MA 95/43/14 AV.2.6.314
MA 96/6 Letter Book 1872–1882
MA 96/6 Letter Book 1882–1890

OFFICE MAORI VALUES

AWMM Repatriation File – Ngati Naho, 2001

TELLING IT LIKE IT IS: THE CALGARY POLICE SERVICE INTERPRETIVE CENTRE

Janet Pieschel

THE CONTEXT

The political and economic climate of the early 1990s saw governments withdrawing from many areas to which they had traditionally provided significant support. The burden of phenomenal debt and deficits impeded their ability to meet the needs of growing systems for health care, social services, and education. At the same time, public concern continued to grow over issues such as child neglect, teen pregnancy, increasing violent crime, substance abuse, suicide, AIDS, unemployment, poverty, pollution, and many other social problems. Institutions such as museums and art galleries, which had been well supported by governments, found themselves struggling to find a voice among the many who were asking politicians for assistance.

Corporations in the United States were quick to realize that healthy communities result in healthier economies, better profits, and an improved public perception of the private-sector innovators who help make the community a better place to live.[1] Their donation programs have increasingly directed funds towards building sustainable communities. Chris Pinney, vice president for corporate citizenship, Canadian Centre for Philanthropy, believes that all financial institutions and most corporations will, like their European counterparts, eventually have to report their social and environmental impacts along with their economic results. Dickenson (1988) noted that American corporations were more supportive of museums than their Canadian counterparts, who saw museums as "dull with little market appeal." Today, although corporations donate less than either the public sector or individuals to the non-profit sector, their contributions are significant.[2]

Canadian museums, which were also impacted by government cutbacks, began to re-examine their purpose within the community and sought more effective ways to conduct their business. Since the early 1980s, there had been much informal discussion at seminars and conferences about the role of museums in the community, the nature of our collections, the interpretations of the artifacts, the nature of our programming, and how we might expand our audiences. Often viewed as elitist and appealing only to the well-educated, it is clear that museums need to attract a wider visitorship, or they will perish. While the democratization of museums (Ames 1992: 37) continues to be an issue within the museum community, it may well be argued that we remain irrelevant to most of the people in the communities we serve.

Museums can change this perception by addressing issues that concern the people within their communities. The social problems outlined above are part of the community experience. By addressing these issues, museums can become an important focal point of community discussion, and an integral part of the mechanism for creating sustainable communities. Moreover, funding may follow from undertaking this new role. The Ketchum Funding Council (2000: 12) maintains that, "Senior managers are ... anxious to ensure that [community] investment is integrated with corporate and business objectives and positioned as a core element of their company's overall commitment to social responsibility." Indeed, John Cleghorn, chairman and CEO of the Royal Bank, noted that, "[a]s corporations redefine their role as corporate citizens, they are becoming more actively engaged to contribute resources and knowledge in order to find innovative solutions to social problems and build a society that is economically, socially and environmentally sustainable" (Ketchum Fund Raising Council 2000: 13).

Stephen Weil (1990), among others, has argued that museums need to re-evaluate their relevancy to their communities. He suggests that a museum collection's greater value might lie in its use for socially worthwhile purposes rather than in its ownership and care. However, he also cautions that by emphasizing an educational role instead of a stewardship responsibility, museums risk losing funding support to educational institutions (Weil 1995).

The mission of the Calgary Police Service Interpretive Centre (CPSIC) was conceived with these issues in mind. Our formative evaluation research indicated that we needed to be a facility that addressed relevant needs in the community. We therefore set forth to develop exhibits and programs which would address some of the tough social problems that are prevalent in our community. Corporate support and the high visitation rates have substantiated our decision.

THE CALGARY POLICE SERVICE INTERPRETIVE CENTRE

The Calgary Police Service Interpretive Centre is a two-thousand-square-metre (six-thousand-square-foot) exhibit and administration space located within the administration building of the Calgary Police Service. It opened in 1995, with a clear mandate to develop exhibits and programs that would be relevant to the community. Senior management of the Calgary Police Service (CPS) saw this as an opportunity to move beyond displays of equipment, weapons, uniforms, and photographs commemorating people and events of Calgary's policing history. Instead, they recognized the potential for explaining the social basis of criminal activity, and altering individual visitor's perspectives about the nature of crime in our community.

Our primary target audience has always been school children. In the early 1990s, at the time that the CPSIC was being planned, Calgary was experiencing a dramatic rise in violent youth crime. In response, the CPS moved away from reactive policing toward a more proactive, community-based approach. Special units were created to address youth issues, and liaisons began working with a number of schools. Police officers recognized that the CPSIC represented an opportunity to develop a facility that focused on the issues of youth and crime. We could be a positive force, educating young people about crime, the consequences of crime, and the poor lifestyle choices that our youth can make.

Our mandate is also to instil a respect for policing and authority. We therefore include an historical component in the CPSIC. In fact, most of the exhibits compare past and present police methods. While many of the issues remain, such as prostitution and substance abuse, the approach to policing has changed in response to evolving social attitudes.

The following reviews three of the exhibits at CPSIC: substance abuse; juvenile prostitution; and domestic abuse, family violence, and healthy relationships. I discuss the intent of the display, its structure, and its effectiveness. I conclude by examining challenges we continue to face, including funding, using docents to discuss sensitive issues, and measuring how receptive our audience is to our message. While the focus of our audience is children in grades five and six, we believe that our mission is applicable to a much broader age range.

THE EXHIBITS

Substance Abuse

Our section on substance abuse addresses a broad range of problems. The misuse of alcohol is interpreted through a graphic depiction of a traffic accident in which alcohol was a causal factor. A photo-mural reveals a collision in which three vehicles have been virtually demolished. A smaller inset shows a dead driver hanging from the door of one of the vehicles. These pictures, taken by investigating officers at the accident scene, deliver a clear message: a drunk driver killed another human being.

The effects of alcohol are reinforced through an opportunity to try a Breathalyzer. Visitors are offered a small amount of alcohol-based mouthwash. A volunteer then assists them in exhaling into a Breathalyzer. A green light blinks if the person has a less than 0.08 per cent alcohol concentration. Most often, the red light is illuminated, reflecting the high concentration of alcohol in the mouthwash. The result usually surprises visitors and underscores the power of alcohol, even in small doses.

The illicit use of drugs has been a policing issue in Calgary since the early 1900s. During the 1960s, the public's attitude towards drug use shifted, as many people began to accept the use of so-called "soft" drugs. Today, Ecstasy is the drug of choice for some people within the Rave culture, and cocaine has become increasingly popular among the young, upper middle class. Although marijuana and hashish have become acceptable to many people, law enforcement agencies see these as the initial steps toward more serious drug use.[3] Police view the use of illegal drugs as a root cause of many other crimes. Heavy users often resort to burglary and armed robbery as sources of ready money needed to support their drug use.

It was a challenge to develop an effective way of portraying the negative impact of drug use. To attract the attention of young visitors, we created *Dead End Streets*, a diorama reconstructing a room in a flop house/crack house. We based it on one we had seen while accompanying police on a tour of such places in Calgary. Our re-creation is visually accurate but lacks the overpowering stench we found in such places.

Our room is filthy and littered with half-eaten doughnuts, discarded chocolate bar wrappers, Styrofoam pop containers from convenience stores, bloody tissues, discarded needles and syringes, cobwebs, and flies. The focal point is a dirty mattress in the middle of the floor where a young female lies unconscious. She is covered with a tattered bedspread, leaving her head and one arm exposed, revealing needle scars from constant injections. A hypodermic needle and a bloody tissue lie near her outstretched hand. As visitors approach the exhibit, they trigger the audio, in which a young man is heard introducing a companion to his new "digs." The companion asks about the girl and learns that she was prostituting herself the night before in order to pay her pimp for the drugs.

The most compelling exhibit within the *Substance Abuse* section is a suicide note that was written by a seventeen-year-old boy from an upper middle class home in Calgary. The letter is displayed in an alcove within the *Dead End Streets* exhibit, and an audio track presents the boy, as portrayed by an actor, reading the letter. He describes his history of drug use as he moved from smoking marijuana and committing petty theft to buy it, to his cocaine addiction and the major break-ins perpetrated to support his expensive habit. In his desperation, he sold his vehicle and stole guns from his father's prized collection, and jewellery from his mother. In the end, remorseful for these activities, he believed that having stolen from his own family he was no longer fit to live. He had shot himself in his parents' basement.

We also collaborated with people outside the CPS to create an effective message. Youth who were new clients at the Alberta Adolescent Recovery Centre prepared a mural reflecting their emotions and views of life affected by their drug use. Dark and sombre, the mural evokes the chaotic thoughts expressed by these people while using drugs.

JUVENILE PROSTITUTION

Most of us live in supportive, emotionally secure family environments. It is hard to imagine situations where children twelve years old, or younger, become involved with prostitution. Yet, in 1995, the CPS estimated that the average age of females entering the sex trade in Calgary was thirteen years of age. It is very difficult to leave prostitution once one has entered the trade. Pimps prey on girls with low self-esteem, using both flattery and abuse to separate them from family, friends, and other support networks. Addiction to drugs keeps many returning to this source of "easy" money. Despite the large amounts of money they may earn, prostitutes generally live lives of destitution, with poor nutrition, poor health (including a myriad of sexually transmitted diseases), and poor living conditions. The life span for prostitutes is much shorter than for the general population.

Creating an exhibit about juvenile delinquency has been one of our greatest challenges. Prostitution is about sex. We needed to find a way of discussing the subject without offending teachers, parents, students, or other members of the public. We developed free-standing, wooden profiles of a pimp and a prostitute that could rotate, allowing visitors to read the messages written on either side. These messages describe the health, social, and psychological consequences of prostitution; the personal characteristics of both a pimp and the type of girl usually seduced by this lifestyle; and a typical come-on of a pimp. A rotating wheel enables visitors to match questions with the unpleasant statistics about prostitution in Calgary. A video, activated by a push-button, presents interviews with girls whom the police have rescued from trick pads (rooms into which girls are locked and forced to have sex with numerous men over the course of a day or evening). Perhaps the most powerful component is the life story of Karen Lewis. Karen ran away from her middle class family and became a prostitute when she was thirteen years old. She left Calgary and moved to Montreal, where a Calgary vice detective found her and began convincing her to move into a "safe house" in Calgary. Unfortunately, she was murdered before she made the move. Karen was eighteen years old. Her murder has never been solved.

DOMESTIC ABUSE, FAMILY VIOLENCE, AND HEALTHY RELATIONSHIPS

There is a strong connection between one's family environment and a person's involvement in criminal activity. Violence in the home is often the root cause of violent behaviour in society. The CPS recognizes this connection and, in 1997, formed the Domestic Conflict Unit. This unit receives approximately nine hundred calls each month regarding domestic abuse and family violence. The police have found children present in 50 per cent of the situations, and believe that the youngsters were probably present in other rooms on many more occasions. Moreover, Jaffe et al. (1990: 113) estimate that one in five children in any classroom are either the subject of abuse, or live in abusive homes. Clearly, abuse and domestic violence are important issues to discuss with school-age visitors to the CPSIC.

It was not easy to create an exhibit about domestic violence. We want all children to understand what constitutes healthy relationships, and that abuse of any kind is neither healthy nor a private, family matter. At the same time, we understood that some of our visitors would be abused children, and that there was a possibility of traumatizing these individuals. Our exhibit design and text were reviewed by child psychologists and other experts to ensure a minimum of negative effects.

As with all of our exhibits, the domestic abuse display is interactive, incorporating both graphic and audio elements. We created three distinct areas: a kitchen, a counselling office, and an outer area concerned with topics associated with domestic violence such as sexual assault and stalking. Structurally, the kitchen is typical of any middle class home. It is cheerful and dominated by bright colours. Inside, the visitor discovers a house divided by anger and fear. The bright colours in one half of the room contrast with darker, gloomier colours in the other side. When visitors turn the knob on the door leading to another room, they hear an abusive argument between a husband and wife over the behaviour of their son. The voices fade and the boy relates his feelings of guilt and inadequacy. This is followed by a narrator who explains that this abusive confrontation could have been a constructive discussion, such as the one that can be heard next. Also located in the kitchen are dishes for dog food and water. Accompanying text explains that the abuse of pets is often an early indicator of growing domestic violence.

A sidewalk linking the kitchen and counselling office is flanked by a colourful mural depicting people of different ages, gender and ethnic backgrounds. In front are three, free-standing profiles. On one side are images of an abused senior, an adult victim, a child victim, and an abuser. Each of the abuse sufferers is accompanied by a list of the symptoms of abuse. The abuse has a list of their "typical" personality traits. The opposite side of the child's profile lists the "rights of a child."

In the counselling office we address subjects associated with domestic abuse. For example, abused spouses often refuse to leave their situation. Police and health professionals become frustrated when they repeatedly assist the same people. Children, especially boys, can grow to resent the spouse who remains in an abusive relationship. Within the office is a puzzle that visitors can assemble to understand the complexity and interconnections of the factors that keep a person from leaving an abusive situation. A filing cabinet that sits against the wall has drawer fronts that lift up. On each drawer's face is a misconception about domestic abuse. The visitor discovers a more accurate explanation by lifting the door.

We recognized that this exhibit could have a profoundly negative effect on children who come from abusive situations. It is imperative that we offer help, as well as information, to visitors in need. A trained volunteer introduces school children to each exhibit at CPSIC. When the domestic abuse exhibit is discussed, the children are told that there is a form in the Counselling Office that they can complete if they have any questions or concerns about family violence and abuse. Each form asks for further comments and if the visitor would like to receive a reply, either directly or through a school counsellor. As they leave the CPSIC, we give each student a yellow business card with the telephone numbers of the Kids' Help Phone and agencies that they can call for help.

Every teacher who visits the CPSIC receives information regarding the symptoms of abuse and the process for handling disclosures of abuse. Teachers in Alberta are required by law to report cases of abuse, even if it is only suspected. We recognized that our exhibit could prompt disclosures and that teachers would often be the adult to whom the student turned for help. We have also found that children have used our question sheet as a means of discussing their own abusive situations.

We handle these disclosures in a variety of ways, depending on the severity of the allegation and the amount of risk the child faces. Often we contact the school and write a letter directly to the child, offering advice and support and providing the telephone number of the Kids' Help Phone. In more serious cases, the disclosures are forwarded to the appropriate police unit, such as the Child at Risk Response Team (in which a police officer works with a social worker), the Domestic Conflict Unit, or the Child Abuse Unit. If the message is ambiguous, a school resource officer is asked to contact the child at school and determine if there is cause for concern.

The disclosures we have received are a clear indication that there is a greater need to educate children about domestic abuse. Because the CPSIC is limited in the number of children we can reach each year, we have now begun to develop outreach programs. Our first, based on domestic abuse, is directed at children in grades four and five. Professionals from the YWCA Family Violence Prevention Centre and the Sheriff King Home were contacted to develop a manual for teachers and to assist the Calgary Police Video Unit to produce a video.

In 2001, Alberta Learning revised the Health and Life Skills curriculum, and incorporated discussions of domestic abuse and family violence in kindergarten through grade twelve. Our material, Helping Children Learn About Healthy Relationships, has been endorsed by the provincial government as support material for this new curriculum. We also sponsor training workshops for grade-four and -five teachers throughout the province, and have initiated discussions with the Faculty of Education at the University of Calgary to provide similar training for education students.

THE CHALLENGES

Fundraising

Fundraising in the early 1990s, when the CPSIC was initiated, was a considerable challenge. Corporations were beginning to redirect their funding from the arts and culture sector to health, education, and social agencies. We approached one corporate foundation twice, once by letter and once in person. The letter received a definitive "no," with the explanation that, in light of government cutbacks, the foundation was focusing on applications that demonstrated a real charitable need; museums need not apply. It was clear that we needed to articulate the social responsibility of our mission. A second appeal, with a better explanation from us, resulted in a very generous donation. A half-million dollars, mostly from corporations, was raised in the ensuing two years, and to date nearly two million dollars have been invested in the facility. Clearly, corporate donors support our community efforts.

The Role of Docents

At the CPSIC, we believe that our exhibits and programs should create awareness of the consequences of antisocial behaviour, and influence young visitors to avoid such lifestyle choices. We continually assess the media through which our message is delivered as we evaluate our effectiveness.

One of our most important media is the corps of volunteers who deliver our programs. The CPSIC has a small salaried staff, including an executive director, an administrator, a secretary/booking clerk, and a part-time gift-shop manager. All other activities are undertaken by volunteers. After eight years of operation, we have developed a strong contingent of seventy volunteers who are phenomenally effective at delivering our programs. Still, problems do arise.

Although we have a core of about twenty-five individuals who have been involved from the CPSIC's inception, the remaining volunteer staff turn over at a rate of 25 per cent every few months. Delivering a consistent message is difficult under such circumstances. Furthermore, some volunteers are reluctant to present a program on family violence or to engage visitors in discussions about the issue. We are attempting to overcome these problems by introducing an automated, life-sized mannequin that can speak and has a limited range of gestures. Dubbed the "Robocop" by the media, he will wear a police uniform and has been named Constable Reilly. He will deliver a consistent message and will initiate discussions with visitors. This does not minimize the importance of human contact provided by the volunteers. However, Reilly may be more effective in opening up conversations, especially on sensitive topics. Because he will be a novelty, we expect that a large proportion of the audience will remember his message. We hope to have Reilly "patrolling the beat" in late 2003.

We have designed three different visitor surveys to help us determine the effectiveness of our educational messages: one for teachers using our forensic science program; one for teachers using the self-guided tour; and one for general visitors. The results so far indicate a consistently high level of satisfaction with our programs. However, this does not tell us whether we have succeeded in convincing youth to avoid drug use and prostitution, or whether we have helped reduce family violence in Calgary. We are currently investigating ways of following up with students over a number of years to determine the long-term effects of our programs.

We have built a pre- and post-test into our outreach programs. Students are given a test before and after the program is delivered. The results indicate what information is retained. Unfortunately, this does not tell us if we have helped prevent anyone from becoming a victim of family violence. We can only hope that the knowledge will help people to make better decisions.

Letters and comments in our Visitor Comment books indicate some of the positive impact of our exhibits. A grade six boy, responding to the Dead End Street, wrote that he "would never, ever let his life end up that way." A young girl concurred, writing that "The drug stand [Dead End Street] is totally gross but I know now what drugs can do. Cool." We also collect approximately 220 visitor surveys each year, the majority of which are completed by teachers and group leaders. A very large proportion (75 per cent) of teachers had visited CPSIC on previous occasions. Other groups return at a much lower rate (20 per cent). Many (46 per cent) of these groups had come following the positive recommendations of their associates.

Our best indicator of success, of course, would be a strong correlation between our programs and a drop in Calgary's crime rate. The Calgary Police Service has noted a decrease in crime following the inception of their community-based policing strategy that focuses on educating the public regarding the prevention and public consequences of criminal activity. It seems reasonable that our educational efforts will have a similarly positive impact. Our programs cannot help but build stronger, safer, and friendlier communities.

ENDNOTES

1. Numerous undated articles and reports in "Corporate Giving in Context" *Center for Nonprofit Management* and www.cnmsocal.org profile corporations that foster community well-being. Peter Manzo (1998) reports that in 1998 corporations donated US$8.2 million to American charities. Paul Clorlery (1999) noted that US$8.9 billion was donated in 1998, excluding corporate foundation giving of US$2.3 and other donations-in-kind, such as marketing and community relations. In fact, corporate giving can become a means of creating a distinctive identity in an increasingly competitive business environment (see *San Francisco Chronicle*, November 22, 2001).
2. Corporate giving in both Canada and the United States appears minimal when compared with other sources. Religious institutions attract the largest number of donors and receive the most money. The impact of corporate giving is greatly enhanced if this segment of the non-profit sector is removed from the analysis.
3. Detectives Pat Tetley and Steve Walton, who have spent most of their careers with the Calgary Police Drug Unit, state that marijuana and hashish were the first drugs used in 100 per cent of the cases in which an individual is now using cocaine, methamphetamines, or heroin. They also note that marijuana and hashish are up to 50 per cent more potent than they were thirty years ago, and that there should be no distinction between "hard" and "soft" drugs. Detectives Tetley and Walton assisted in the development of the Dead End Streets exhibit.

REFERENCES

Ames, Michael M.
    1992   Dilemmas of the practical anthropologist. In Michael M. Ames (Ed.), *Cannibal tours and glass boxes: The anthropology of museums* (pp. 25–37). Vancouver: University of British Columbia Press.

Clorlery, Paul
    1999   Article in *The Nonprofit Times*, August 1999.

Dickenson, Victoria
    1988   *Management for Canadian Museums*. Background Paper for Policy Working Group. Ottawa: Communications Canada.

Ketchum Fund Raising Council
    2000   *Ketchum Philanthropic Trends*. Toronto.

Jaffee, Peter G., David A. Wolfe and Susan Wilson
    1990   *Children of battered women*. London, Ont.: Sage Publications.

Manzo, Peter
    1998   Corporate giving recaps multiple rewards. *The Los Angeles Business Journal* 20(6): 16–22.

Weil, Stephen
    1990   *Rethinking the museum and other meditations*. Washington: Smithsonian Institution Press.
    1995   *A Cabinet of curiosities: inquiries into museums and their prospects*. Washington Smithsonian Institution Press.

CONTRIBUTORS

RUTH J. ABRAM is the president and founder of the Lower East Side Tenement Museum, New York City, New York. With master's degrees in social welfare (Heller School at Brandeis University) and American history (New York University), Abram understands history as a tool for understanding and a basis for social change.

STEPHEN H. BAUMANN is vice president of education and programs at Liberty Science Center, Jersey City, New Jersey. His work focuses on the ways that the resources of a science centre are leveraged to support mediated, staff-facilitated science-learning experiences. He moved to Liberty Science Center in 1999 from The Franklin Institute in Philadelphia, where he was director of Educational Technology for six years. With a career that started as an elementary school teacher, he received his B.S. from the University of Pennsylvania and M.S. in science education from the University of Virginia. Publications that feature his contributions to the science-centre field have appeared in *Dimensions of the Association of Science-Technology Centers*, *Museum News of the American Association of Museums*, the *Journal of Museum Education*, and *Technological Horizons in Education*.

BETH CARTER has been a curator of ethnology with the Glenbow Museum for over fifteen years, and has worked on several major exhibitions, including *The Spirit Sings: Artistic Traditions of Canada's First Peoples*, *Many Faces, Many Paths: Art of Asia*, and *Head to Toe: Personal Adornment around the World*. She has a Bachelor of Arts degree from the University of British Columbia and a master's degree in Social Anthropology from the University of Cambridge. She worked as the project coordinator for the *Nitsitapiisinni: Our Way of Life* gallery, which opened in 2001.

GERALD T. CONATY received his B.A. (Hons) from the University of Alberta, his M.A. from Memorial University of Newfoundland, and his Ph.D. in archaeology from Simon Fraser University. He has been on teams for exhibits such as *Nitsitapiisinni: Our Way of Life*, *The Fur Trade in Western Canada*, *Warriors: A Global Journey Through Five Centuries*, *Growing Up and Away: Childhood in Western Canada* and *Powerful Images: Portrayals of Native America*. Dr. Conaty has written over thirty articles and books. He is currently senior curator of ethnology at the Glenbow Museum, and assistant adjunct professor, Department of Archaeology, University of Calgary.

JOANNE DICOSIMO is president and chief executive officer of the Canadian Museum of Nature, Ottawa, Ontario. Since her appointment in 1997, Ms. DiCosimo has worked to increase the public value of this national museum, and her article documents one of the major renewal strategies undertaken. Prior to this, DiCosimo served for nine years as executive director of the Manitoba Museum of Man and Nature. Ms. DiCosimo holds a master's degree in Public Administration degree from Harvard University and a Bachelor of Arts (Honours) degree from the University of Winnipeg. Her heritage awards include the Province of Manitoba's Prix Award (1997), honorary life memberships in the Manitoba Museum (1997) and the Association of Manitoba Museums (1998), and the Queen's Jubilee Medal for service to the museum community (2003).

MICHÈLE GALLANT is a museum professional who has been involved in education work since 1986. Since joining Glenbow Museum in Calgary in 1993, her work has focused on building innovative partnerships between museums, schools, and community members including writers, dancers, musicians, and visual artists. By allowing visitors to explore the museum in multiple ways, she believes that individuals will find deep personal meaning within the museum's collections. Since 1996, she has been the education coordinator for the award-winning Glenbow Museum School.

ROBERT R. JANES is a museum/heritage consultant. He was founding director of the Prince of Wales Northern Heritage Centre (1976–86), the founding executive director of the Science Institute of the Northwest Territories

(1986–89), and president and CEO of the Glenbow Museum (1989–2000). He holds a Ph.D. in archaeology from the University of Calgary, where he is currently an adjunct professor. Janes is the author of three books and over eighty articles in the fields of archaeology, anthropology, museology and management, and is currently the chief editor of the Journal of Museum Management and Curatorship.

EMLYN H. KOSTER has been Liberty Science Center's president and CEO since 1996. Born in Egypt and growing up in England, he came to Canada in 1971 to earn his Ph.D. in geology from the University of Ottawa. Initially in academia and research, his career focus shifted to museums in 1986. Before moving to the U.S.A., he was director of Alberta's Royal Tyrrell Museum of Palaeontology and director general of the Ontario Science Centre. Board appointments have included the Geological Association of Canada (president, 1996–97), Giant Screen Theater Association (vice president, 2003–04), as well as the Challenger Center for Space Science Education and Association of Science-Technology Centers (1993–2001). Current appointments include the Leadership Council of the United Nations Association of the U.S.A., the Board of Prosperity New Jersey, and the Advisory Council of the Metropolitan Waterfront Alliance serving the New York City region. Since joining the museum field, his speaking engagements and publications have focused on its social and environmental responsibility. He is the recipient of the 2003 John Cotton Dana Award from the New Jersey Association of Museums.

GILLIAN KYDD is a visionary and somewhat rebellious educator who co-founded the ChevronTexaco Open Minds and Campus Calgary School Programs in 1993, in her role as a science consultant with the Calgary Board of Education. For the following ten years with the school district, she was the director of the programs. Kydd is presently working with other cities that are using the Open Minds model. She believes passionately that we must take learning beyond the classroom walls into the rich life of the community.

JANET PIESCHEL received her Master's degree in history from the Uni-versity of Calgary and spent several years self-employed as a historical resource consultant. She was employed by the Glenbow Museum, as an archivist, for three years before going to work for the Calgary Police Service in 1990 to manage the police archives and develop the police interpretive centre. Pieschel is currently executive director of the Calgary Police Service Interpretive Centre and Archives.

190   CONTRIBUTORS

SUSAN POINTE directs the McMullen Art Gallery at the University of Alberta Hospital, the Hospital's art collection, and the Artists on the Wards program. Pointe has worked in the museum sector for twelve years with both large and small heritage and art institutions. She is a graduate of the Master's of Museum Studies Program at the University of Toronto.

GLENN C. SUTTER received his M.Sc. from the University of Manitoba and a Ph.D. from the University of Regina. He acted as coordinator of the Canadian Global Change Program for the Royal Society of Canada from 1988 to 1992. He has been curator of ornithology and human ecology at the Royal Saskatchewan Museum since 1997 and adjunct professor of biology at the University of Regina since 1998. As a researcher, he is interested in all aspects of sustainability and how organisms and systems respond to stress. As a curator, he is responsible for *The Human Factor* exhibit, which examines regional and global issues associated with human activity.

PAUL TAPSELL is a descendant of the Maori tribes, Te Arawa and Tainui. A former curator of the Rotorua Museum in New Zealand, Oxford doctoral scholar, and post-doctoral fellow at Australian National University, in 2000 he became the first director-Maori of the Auckland War Memorial Museum, and lectures at the University of Auckland.

DOUGLAS WORTS has been a museologist for more than twenty years, employed as an educator/planner for most of that time with the Art Gallery of Ontario in Toronto. His specializations in audience research and the development of experimental interpretive strategies (including computers, audio, video, text and feedback systems) have led to extensive publications and presentations in Canada, the United States, Europe, Australia and New Zealand. In 1997, he became an associate of Leadership for Environment and Development (LEAD International), which is a worldwide network of professionals who share an interest in sustainability. Since then his research and writing have been focused on how museums can best foster a "culture of sustainability."

INDEX

A

Abram, Ruth, 187
    "History is as History Does: The Evolution of a Mission-Driven Museum," 19–42
Acevedo, Georgina, 30
Alberta Foundation for the Arts, 120, 121
Alberta Learning, 183
Alliance of Natural History Museums of Canada, 68
American Association of Museums (AAM), 85, 105
American Heart Association, 103
Ames, Michael, 2, 43, 44, 45, 176
Art Gallery of Ontario, 147
Association of Science-Technology Centers, 89, 105
Atlantic Health System, 103
Auckland War Memorial Museum
    Human Remains Database Project, 167–68
    human-remains policy, 167
    Maori ancestral remains, collection and return of, 153–69
    Maori-related governance policies, 166

B

Bamfield Marine Station, 60

Bardwell, L., 137
Baribeau, Thérèse, 147
Barker, Richard, 87
Barkley, Bill, 9
Baron, Dave, 68
Barrett, Richard, 87
Barrow, T., 157
Baumann, Stephen H., 187
    "Liberty Science Center in the United States: A Mission Focussed on External Relevance," 85–111
BBH Exhibits / Clear Channel Entertainment, 105
Belich, J., 161
Bennett, Tony, 2, 45
Blair Fraser Exhibits, Ltd., 137
Block, Peter, 8, 10, 11, 12
Boschee, Jerr, 107
Breau, Anne, 147
Brink, Jack, 44
British Museum, 2, 157–58
Brousseau, Francine, 86, 88
Brown, Joseph Epes, 4
Bullock, Alan, 5
Burton, Christine, 5

C

Calgary Foundation, 71

Calgary Police Service Interpretive Centre, 175–86
    docents, role of, 184–85
    Domestic Abuse exhibit, 181–83
    fundraising challenges, 183–84
    Juvenile Prostitution exhibit, 180–81
    mission, 177
    outreach programs, 183
    Substance Abuse exhibit, 178–80
California Museum of Science and Industry, 88
California Science Center, 88
Cameron, Duncan, 2, 3, 10, 46
Canadian Association of Science Centres (CASC), 89
Canadian Centre for Philanthropy, 175
Canadian Heritage Information Network, 68
Canadian Millennium Partnership Program, 121
Canadian Museum of Civilization, 44
Canadian Museum of Nature (CMN)
    Collections Development Plan, 61
    environmental issues and, 64–65, 66, 67
    funding and support, 65
    international role, 64
    model of national service, development of, 59–70
    public policy and, 64
    Rideau River Biodiversity Project, 67
    Saskatchewan Waterway Project, 67
    social responsibility and, 59–60
    technology plan, 67–68
    and the Working Group on Museums and Sustainable Communities, 131, 147
Canadian Museums Association (CMA), 61, 86, 147–48
Capital Health Authority, 123
Carbonne, Stan, 86
Carter, Beth, 187–88
    "Our Story in Our Words: Diversity and Equality in the Glenbow Museum," 43–58
Caruth, James, 159
Casey, Dawn, 46, 88
Cheeseman, Thomas, 158–59
Chelog, C., 133
Chevron Calgary Resources (CCR), 71
Chevron Canada Resources, 82–83
ChevronTexaco Corporation, 71
City University of New York, 33
civic engagement, 11, 41
Cleghorn, John, 176
Clinebell, H.J., 141
Cobb, C., 133
Cochrane, Cathy, 79–80
Conaty, Gerald T., 188
    "Introduction," 1–15
    "Our Story in Our Words: Diversity and Equality in the Glenbow Museum," 43–58
Conservation Company, The, 99
Costanza, R., 142
Covey, Stephen, 87, 105
Craig, Eric, 160
Crane Bear, Clifford, 51
Curruth, James, 160

D

Daly, Herman, 134
Dana, John Cotton, 10, 85, 107, 108
Day Rider, Rosie, 47
"Declaration on the Importance and Value of Universal Museums," 13
Dees, Gregory, 107
Derbyshire, P., 53
Devonian Foundation, 73
Dickenson, Victoria, 176
DiCosimo, Joanne, 68, 188
    "One National Museum's Work to Develop a New Model of National Service: A Work in Progress," 59–70
Dierking, Lynn D., 53, 75
District Six Museum, The, 38
Duckworth, Eleanor, 76
Dumouchel, Catherine, 147
Duncan, J.A., 113

E

Eades, Colin, 62–63
Economy, Peter, 107
Elgin, Duane, 12
Emerson, Jed, 107
environment/environmental stewardship, 10, 14, 64–65, 66, 67, 86, 88

Environment Canada, 147
Epps, Renee, 29–32
Exploratorium, San Francisco, 89

F
Falk, John, 53, 75, 91
Fforde, C., 157, 158, 162
First Nations
    development of *Nitsitapiisinni*
        exhibit with Glenbow Museum,
        43, 46–56
    relations with Canadian museums,
        43–46
First Nations Gallery, 44
Florence Museum, 159
Ford Foundation, 38
Franklin Institute, 88
Frick Museum, 26
Friends of the University Hospital, 114, 120, 121

G
Gallant, Michèle, 188–89
    "Engaging Young Minds and Spirits:
        The Glenbow Museum School,"
        71–84
Gardner, Howard, 76
Gejdos, Dave, 138
Gibb, James G., 46
Glenbow Museum, 43–57
    Nitsitapiisinni exhibit, 43, 46–56
    The Spirit Sings exhibit, political/legal
        issues, 44
    team partnership with Blackfoot
        people, 43, 46–56
Glenbow Museum School, 71–84
    approach to teaching, 73–74
    ChevronTexaco Open Minds School
        Program, 72–73
    collaboration with teachers, 74–75
    program benefits and impact, 76–82
    program description, 71–73
    role in community, 82–84
Glickman, M., 133
Graf, Britta, 35–36
Graham, George, 163–64
Graham, K., 53
Grasset, Constance D., 2, 45
Grove, Richard, 10

Gulag Museum, 38, 39–40
Gunvordahl, Terry, 54
Gurian, Elaine, 107

H
Handy, Charles, 11, 12
Harrison, Julia D., 44
Harvard University, Kennedy School of
    Government, 85, 106
Harvie, Donald, 73, 83
Head-Smashed-In Buffalo Jump, 44
Hector, James, 158
Hill, Tom, 44
History Channel, The, 28
Holling, C.S., 134
Hollinger, Michael, 97, 98
hospital art galleries, 113. *See also*
    McMullen Art Gallery, University of
    Alberta Hospital
Hume, Christopher, 4

I
Ignatieff, Michael, 45–46
indigenous peoples, 15. *See also* First
    Nations; Maori ancestral remains
Insectarium de Montréal, 68
International Coalition of Historic Site
    Museums of Conscience, 38–41
International Council of Museums
    (ICOM), 86, 148

J
Jacobson, Anita, 21
Jaffe, Peter G., 181
Janes, Robert, 44, 50, 189
    "Introduction," 1–15
Johnson & Johnson, 103

K
Kabat-Zinn, Jon, 10
Kaplan, S., 137
Kawharu, I.H., 154, 161, 164
Keech, Pamela, 27
Kerr, Irene, 54
Ketchum Funding Council, The, 176
Kilvert, Elizabeth, 147
Kimmelman, Michael, 108
King, Charles, 96

194　INDEX

Kingwell, Mark, 6
Koster, Emlyn H., 189
 "Liberty Science Center in the United States: A Mission Focused on External Relevance," 85–111
Krahn, Ed, 68
Kydd, Gillian, 189–90
 "Engaging Young Minds and Spirits: The Glenbow Museum School," 71–84

L

Landry, Johanne, 68
Leahy, Stephen, 86
Lein, Dale, 121
Leonard, George, 10, 12
Leopold, Aldo, 136
Li, Florence, 36
Liberation War Museum, 38
Liberty Science Center
 Abbott Partnership Program, 91–96
 education programs, 90, 97–105
 funding and support, 93, 105–8
 introduction to, 88–91
 mission, 90, 107
 partnerships, 103
 social responsibility and, 86, 107–8
 technologies, use of, 91, 101–4
Liboiron, Linda, 147
Lightspeed Design Group, 97
Long, Steve, 27–28
Lopez, Barry, 14
Louvre Museum, 2
Lovelock, J.E., 138
Lower East Side Tenement Museum, 19–42
 community connections, 33
 docent-led tours, 23–24
 funding and support, 33, 37
 good-neighbour program, 33–34
 Immigrant Programs Department, 29
 immigrant tenant apartments, 31–32
 Institute for Directors of Historic Sites plans, 41
 and the International Coalition of Historic Site Museums of Conscience, 38–41
 Lower East Side Community Preservation Project, 36
 M.A.–granting program, 33
 mission, 19, 24, 29
 multi-lingual services, 26, 29, 31, 32, 34, 36
 Networth program, 26
 organization-wide diversity, 32–34
 program evaluation criteria, 28
 services for visitors with disabilities, 34
 staff training and involvement, 29–30, 35–36
 usable past concept, 19–20, 24–26, 36–37
 visitor experience, 26–29
Lyndhurst, 26

M

Maori ancestral remains, collection and repatriation of, 153–69
Marten, G.G., 134, 135, 143
McAlpine, Don, 68
McGhee, Robert, 47
McGillivray, Bruce, 69
McKean, Barbara, 147
McKibben, Bill, 3, 7
McLoed, M., 117
McMullen, William, 114
McMullen Art Gallery, University of Alberta Hospital, 113–27
 artists-on-the-wards program, 117–22
 awareness campaign and new program design, 116–17
 educators and program staff, 124–25
 funding and support, 114, 120, 121
 hands-on programs, 126
 responding to community needs, 126–27
Memoria Abierta, 38
Mid-Atlantic Surgical Associates, 103
Moore, Mark, 106
Muir, John, 136
Murphy, Michael, 10, 12
Museum of Anthropology, University of British Columbia, 43
Museum of Modern Art (MOMA), 4
Museum of Science, Boston, 88

INDEX 195

Museum of Science and Industry, Chicago, 88

N
Nadasdy, Paul, 45
Native peoples. *See* First Nations; Maori ancestral remains
Natural History League (NHL), 69
Natural Sciences and Engineering Research Council of Canada (NSERC), 61
Naylor, Bruce, 68
New Brunswick Museum, 68
New Jersey Department of Education, 92, 94–95
New York Society of Association Executives, 92
Ngata, Sir Apirana, 163
Nicks, Trudy, 44

O
Ontario Science Centre, 89
Open Society Institute, 38
Orchiston, D.W., 155, 156
Orr, D.W., 140

P
Paris Natural History Museum, 158
Parston, Greg, 87
Petit, J.R., 142
Pieschel, Janet, 190
  "Telling It Like It Is: The Calgary Police Service Interpretive Centre," 175–86
Pinney, Chris, 175
Playwright's Theatre of New Jersey, 98
Pointe, Susan, 190
  "Is Art Good for You?", 113–27
Postman, Neil, 13
Prince of Wales Northern Heritage Centre, The, 44
Pruneau, Diane, 147

R
Rafferty, Pauline, 68
Rees, W., 133
relevance concept, 86–88, 105, 123–24
repatriation, 13. *See also* Maori ancestral remains

Rideau River Biodiversity Project, 67
Rifkin, Jeremy, 5
Robley, H.G., 156, 157
Rockefeller Foundation, 38
Rockwood Lane, M., 117
Rosenzweig, Roy, 24
Rowe, S., 131, 142
Royal Bank, 176
Royal Botanical Garden, Hamilton, 60–61, 147
Royal British Columbia Museum, 43, 68
Royal College of Surgeons, 157
Royal Saskatchewan Museum, 68, 137, 147
  The Human Factor exhibit, 131, 137–42
Royal Tyrell Museum, 68
Russell-Ciardi, Maggie, 29

S
Samuels, M., 117
Sanderson, E.W., 138
Saskatchewan Waterway Project, 67
Schiele, Bernard, 91
science centres/museums. *See* Canadian Museum of Nature (CMN); Liberty Science Center
Scott, Carol, 5
Sevcenko, Liz, 25
Shands Medical Center, Gainesville, Florida, 117, 122
Shell Canada Ltd., 44
Sheppard, P., 135
Sheriff King Home, 183
Siegel, Michael, 96
Silverman, L., 137
Simons, Jeffrey, 106
Simons, Robin, 106
Skramstad, Harold, 86
Slakter, D., 137
Slave House, Senegal, 38
Smith, Monica L., 45
Smithsonian Institute, 86, 159
Snider, Katherine, 34–35
social change, and museums, 131, 136–37, 142–47
social entrepreneurship, 106–7
social equity, 11, 20
social relevance, 86–88, 105, 123–24
social responsibility, 1–14, 59–60, 86, 105–9, 154

Société des musées québécois, 86
Stapp, C.B., 146
Staricoff, R.L., 113
Steckel, Richard, 106
Stocking, G.W., 162
sustainability / sustainable cultural development
    challenges, 8–9, 129–32, 132–37
    The Human Factor exhibit, insights from, 137–43
    museums, role of, 130, 131, 136–37, 142–47
Sutter, Glenn C., 190
    "Negotiating a Sustainable Path: Museums and Societal Therapy," 129–51

T

Tallow, Mae, 50
Tanen, Norman, 106
Tansey, William A., III, 101
Tapsell, Paul, 190
    "Out of Sight, Out of Mind: Human Remains at the Auckland Museum – *Te Papa Whakahiku*", 153–73
Task Force on First Peoples and Museums, 44
Tenement Museum. *See* Lower East Side Tenement Museum
Terezin Memorial, Czech Republic, 38
Thelen, David, 24
Toronto Star, 4
Tothill, C., 159, 160
Trigger, Bruce, 44
Trombley, Stephen, 5
Trust for Mutual Understanding, 38

U

UNESCO, 129
United Nations
    global population growth rates, 133
    Our Common Future (Brundtland report), 130, 135

Université de Moncton, 147
University of Alberta Hospital, McMullen Art Gallery, 113–27
University of Cambridge, 157
University of Edinburgh, 157
University of Oxford, 157
Urban Museum Studies Program, City University of New York, 33
U.S. National Center for Nonprofit Boards, 107
U.S. National Park Service, 38

V

von Haast, Julius, 158

W

Wackernagel, M., 133
Walker, R.J., 154, 164
Wanuskewin Heritage Site, 44
Weasel Head, Frank, 50
Weil, Stephen, 85, 88, 146, 176–77
Weschler, Lawrence, 45
Whalley, George, 10
Wilber, Ken, 6, 7, 11
Wilson, E.O., 143
Winter, D.D., 135, 141
Woodhouse, Mark B., 7
Workhouse, The, 38
Working Group on Museums and Sustainable Communities, 131, 147–48
Worts, Douglas, 88, 190–91
    "Negotiating a Sustainable Path: Museums and Societal Therapy," 129–51

Y

Yukon Berengia Interpretive Centre, 68
YWCA Family Violence Prevention Centre, 183

Z

Zernan, John, 7

www.ingramcontent.com/pod-product-compliance
Lightning Source LLC
Chambersburg PA
CBHW070805230426
43665CB00017B/2498